The life of
SIR DENIS HENRY
Catholic Unionist

A.D. McDONNELL

ULSTER HISTORICAL FOUNDATION

First published 2000
by the Ulster Historical Foundation
12 College Square East, Belfast, BT1 6DD

ISBN 0-901905-94-1

Typeset by the Ulster Historical Foundation
Printed by Betaprint
Cover and Design by Dunbar Design

This book has received support from the Cultural Diversity Programme of
the Community Relations Council which aims
to encourage acceptance and understanding of cultural diversity.
The views expressed do not necessarily reflect those of the
NI Community Relations Council.

Contents

ACKNOWLEDGEMENTS

I should like to thank all those who have helped in the writing of this book. I am very grateful to the late Mr John Magee who many years ago stimulated my interest in the period of the 1918 General Election in Ulster out of which arose this study of Denis Henry. I wish to acknowledge the kindness and courtesy which I received from the History Department of what was formerly known as St Joseph's College of Education (now St. Mary's College, Belfast), and convey my long-standing appreciation to Mr Seamus Bennett and Brother Michael Gleeson for the help they gave me when attending St Mary's Grammar School, Belfast. Dr Sydney Elliott of Queen's University Belfast was a source of encouragement to me during my doctoral research, while the late Lord Lowry of Crossgar and the late Major Hall-Thompson helped me to establish a vital link with the Henry family, on whose behalf the late Sir James Henry QC CMG MC TD added considerably to my knowledge of his father's work. I am indebted to Mr Graham Mawhinney and his wife for the generosity and kindness with which they received me during my research in Draperstown; Mr William Roulston for his genealogical skills; and to Dr Eamon Phoenix for his sustained support during the last twelve months.

For permission to consult valuable source material, I wish to record my thanks to several individuals and to the staffs of the following depositories and libraries; Mrs Hazel Legge; Dr John Emberson; Mr Ian Battersby, Archivist, Mount St. Mary's College; His Honour Judge Hart QC; Professor Keith Jeffery; Dr Brian Trainor; the National Library of Ireland; the Linenhall Library; Belfast Central Library; Queen's University Library; Queen's Law Library; and the Deputy Keeper of the Public Record Office of Northern Ireland.

Early life and involvement in politics

DENIS STANISLAUS HENRY was born on 7 March 1864 in Cahore, Draperstown, Co. Derry. His father, James Henry, was quite prosperous by the standards of his peers, being described at various times as a farmer, landlord or businessman. James Henry's first wife was Mary McNamee, and his second was Ellen Kelly, a daughter of a Doctor Kelly from Derry who practised in Draperstown for ten years. Writing in 1993, Eoin Walsh speculated that this was a mixed marriage, 'but I am open to correction on this point,' a reservation confirmed by the marriage certificates which identify James Henry and his wives as Catholic.[1] James Henry had five children by his first marriage; a son, James, and four daughters. Denis Henry was one of seven children by his father's second marriage.[2]

1

Enthusiasm for religious and legal affairs was a feature of the Henry family. Denis' eldest brother, Thomas, joined the Marists, and died some years before Denis' own demise in 1925. Another brother, William, became Rector of the Jesuit novitiate of St Stanislaus College in Tullamore. Both of Denis' sisters took religious vows as well: Margaret, as Sister Mary Berchman, with the Loreto Convent in Omagh, while Rose joined the Dominicans in Blackrock, Dublin, as Sister Mary Paul.[3]

The Henry family's interest in legal matters was evident in the careers of Denis' two remaining brothers. Patrick Joseph, known locally as 'Attorney Henry', became a solicitor and died at the family home, the 'Rath', on 9 April 1919, aged 53. Alexander Patterson Henry began as a solicitor and then became a Registrar in the Chancery Division of the High Court of Justice of Northern Ireland. He was born on 23 December 1868, and died on 3 September 1935.[4] Denis Henry's father, James, died on 22 October 1880, aged 67, and his mother, Ellen, passed away on 3 October 1908, in her eightieth year.[5] The will of James Henry provides some testimony as to his standing in the community. Described in his will as a 'merchant', James bequeathed to his 'Dearly beloved wife' Ellen, for her natural life, 'the dwelling house in which I reside in Cahore, with offices, house, yard garden and field.' Among the various sums of money left to his family, James granted Denis the figure of £400, a sizeable amount, bearing in mind that thirty years hence this was to be the first official salary for Westminster MPs.[6] During an interview with the late Sir James Henry in 1979, he described his father as a 'prosperous farmer', while Denis Henry's school register in Draperstown lists his father's occupation as 'Landlord'.[7] Nothing alters the fact that James Henry lived comfortably, and was able to assist his family in their educational upbringing essential for their chosen careers. Something, too, is known of the Henry family ties with Draperstown and the surrounding area. Eoin Walsh, a nephew of Louis J. Walsh, Denis Henry's Sinn Fein opponent in the South Derry election of 1918, revealed that Denis was 'a cousin of my mother, daughter of

Michael Dougan and Mary McNamee'.[8] The Henrys were also cousins of the Henrys of Maghera, whose father Peter was the famous Royal Naval Surgeon who served in the Napoleonic Wars, and who formed part of a medical team who later tended to Bonaparte on St. Helena. Coincidentally, one of Peter Henry's sons was also named Alexander, and was known as 'Attorney Henry' in Maghera.[9]

Draperstown had an interesting history, forming part of the Ulster Plantation by the great London companies. Draperstown was originally known as 'The Town of the Cross' or, in Irish, 'Baile na Croise'. Lying in a valley between the Sperrin Mountains to the west, and Slieve Gullion to the south-east in the Ballinascreen division, the name of Draperstown was given to 'The Cross' in 1818.[10] In the years before the Famine, the Drapers' Company appointed a new surveyor, William Joseph Booth, who designed the towns of Moneymore and Draperstown. Booth, 'a highly accomplished draughtsman and topographical artist', completed the bulk of his work by 1845.[11] Both towns had a symmetrical group of buildings, with a market-place in the centre flanked by an inn and a dispensary. On either side of these central public buildings were to be terrace houses. The triangular green was to be enlarged, and a school to be built at the cross.[12] In 1832 a Deputation from the Drapers' Company reported that the situation of Draperstown was 'admirably calculated to render it a market town of first-rate importance in that part of Ireland'.[13] However, the Famine hit the Drapers' Company Estates, with one-third of revenues being lost. Famine relief works resulted in the building of roads, draining of lands, erection of walls, and the planting of hedges, as pasture replaced arable land as the commonest type of farming.[14] The process of draining land began in 1847, when 513 acres were drained at a cost of £5 per acre, paid for by the Company. Between 1847–53, over 2,000 acres had been drained, the Drapers having contributed £8,000 to the scheme.[15] The 1850s saw Draperstown benefit from a railway connection to Randalstown, and the growing prosperity of Draperstown attracted people to settle in houses which were, like the railway, 'in a forward state'. When the inhabitants requested a market for the sale of pork, the Company accommodated them. A Deputation in 1862 observed that Draperstown was 'foremost among the market towns' of the 'flourishing' county of Londonderry, and the tenants of the Company pronounced themselves 'blessed', so 'efficiently, benevolently and unbiased' was the management of the estate. The Deputation noted that, 'Stimulated by the works of improvement at Draperstown, the holder of the Townland of Cahore had nearly rebuilt the whole of his part of the town, setting the houses back, and giving it a most respectable appearance.'[16]

Denis Henry's education provided him with a variety of experiences and much academic success. For a while he attended the local National School, Draperstown School for Boys, the school records showing that Denis enrolled as a Catholic pupil in a school which had some Presbyterian boys as well.[17] After Draperstown, Denis attended the Marist College in Dundalk, subsequently accompanying his brother Patrick – who was next to him in age – to the Jesuit college of Mount St Mary's near Chesterfield, enrolling on 14 September 1878. The college magazine, the 'Mountaineer', did not commence until 1902, so it is not possible to find any reference to Henry before that date. However, his name does not appear in the Jesuit Academy programmes (which list prize-winners), suggesting that Henry was an average student. The choice of Mount St Mary's can perhaps be explained by the fact that Denis' uncle, Father William Henry, S.J., who had died in the 1850s, had also attended the school. A noteworthy aside is that the poet, Gerard Manley Hopkins, taught Classics at the college, sometime between 1876–1879, his term overlapping with Denis Henry's.[18] Henry's potential in legal affairs only became apparent following his work as a law student at Queen's College, Belfast, where he achieved the distinction of winning every available law scholarship possible, as well as winning other exhibitions and prizes.[19] In spite of his academic commitments, Henry still found

4

time to make friends with fellow-students. Residing at lodgings in Donegall Pass in Belfast, Henry also enjoyed leisure time to the full.[20] It was against this background that in 1885, at the age of twenty-one, Henry was called to the Irish Bar, and thus embarked on a career which was to reach its climax during the most turbulent period in this country's history.

Like so many prominent lawyers of this era, Denis Henry became closely involved with politics, and even though the evidence is sparse, it is possible to comment with some conviction as to why and when Henry endorsed the Unionist cause. Sir James Henry, when discussing this aspect of his father's career, was adamant that his father did not share the predictable tendency to identify one's own religious persuasion with a particular political viewpoint:

> He felt very strongly that religion and politics were totally different…that one had no obligation to follow the majority over politics…if a Protestant, there was no obligation on one to be a Unionist…and in reverse, he could not see why a Catholic could not be a Unionist.[21]

On the basis of what material is available, it can be said with assurance that Henry was no late convert to the Unionist cause, a point which emerges from the testimony of his supporters during the North Tyrone election of 1906. Professor Dickey of Magee College, an acquaintance of the Henry family, referred to Henry's support for the Unionist Sir Thomas Lea in 1895, and spoke of the Henry family's opposition to the Land League.[22] In 1895, at the age of thirty-two, Henry stood on the election platforms of two Unionists. Moreover, in a speech at Plumbridge on 8 January 1906, Henry rounded off a strong defence of the Union by reminding his audience that he and his family had at one time been Liberals, but had declined to go with Mr Gladstone when he took up Home Rule. He then added that he had been an opponent of Home Rule for the previous twenty years, which is approximate to the time of Gladstone's first Home Rule Bill of 1886.[23] It is worth recalling the political impact that Home Rule had on the Liberal Party, so in this context it is unremarkable that the Henry family should reassess their political allegiance. James Henry and his family had benefited from the Union, and in this regard provide support for one of the traditional Ulster-based economic arguments for resisting Home Rule. Ulster businessmen formed themselves into a committee of the Ulster Unionist Council, 'and there was considerable evidence of the possible adverse effects that home rule would have upon the Irish economic and financial world.'[24] Political advancement seems an unlikely motivation in Denis Henry's Unionism. In 1886, he was only twenty-two, and an unknown. While he had demonstrable academic ability and undoubted legal potential, he was still a newcomer to the Irish Bar, and was hardly in any position to benefit from political advancement as a consequence of his adherence to Unionism. During the 1906 North Tyrone contest, one speaker at Ardstraw declared that Henry had always been a Unionist and his father before him. Perhaps Henry's own educational experiences played a role in shaping his political outlook, for during this election campaign he voiced his disapproval of a sectarian university, saying 'Mixing was good for everyone, as it broadened their views and let them see that other people held as honest opinions as themselves.'[25]

If Denis Henry experienced no inner conflict over his religion and politics, how did his contemporaries react to his apparently contradictory pose? There are indications that Denis remained close to his family, indicated by the fact that his brother, Patrick Joseph, appointed him executor of his will on 21 August 1903, bequeathing to Denis 'all property, subject to the payment of £1000 to Alexander Patterson'.[26] Moreover, Alexander would later act as Denis' Private Secretary when he became Lord Chief Justice in 1921. The people of Draperstown received Henry well, and Sir James Henry revealed how his father was able to go into the village and socialise with everyone and engage in amicable conversation. As subsequent testimony will show, this ability to mix with others was to become something of a Henry trademark and, combined with his early declaration for the

Union and his legal ability, made his Catholic Unionism more readily acceptable as time progressed. Sir James was unaware of any family unease over his father's Unionism, and remarked that Denis' brothers visited his residence in 28 Fitzwilliam Square, Dublin, where Denis lived while practising at the Four Courts.[27]

One of the few surviving documents of Denis Henry is a set of figures, undated, showing a detailed breakdown of the electorate in the South Derry area:

POLLING DISTRICTS	UNIONISTS	NATIONALISTS
Agivevy	673	165
Bellaghy	841	1335
Draperstown	445	2303
Garnagh	1189	775
Kilrea	1580	748
Magherafelt	2507	1389
Maghera	2020	2205
Moneymore	1870	1183
	10101	10101

Unionist majority 1024

The earliest record of Denis Henry's involvement in an electoral contest on behalf of the Unionists came during the 1895 general election, when he supported the Unionist nominee, Sir Thomas Lea, in South Derry – a seat which Henry himself was to capture in 1916. The poll in the constituency was described as 'the largest and most exhaustive ever made', with Lea defeating his rival by 4,485 votes to 4,068.[28] The nature of the result, greeted with bonfires and torchlight processions in Belfast, has some relevance here, for it appears that Denis Henry was destined to have some involvement in the most exciting contests. By a strange twist of fate, the unsuccessful opponent was W.H. Dodd, who was to face Henry in the 1906 election in North Tyrone.[29]

Henry also expressed an interest in the East Donegal contest of 1895, and his appearance on the platform of the Unionist,

Emmerson Tennent Herdman, prompted this response from the Nationalist newspaper, the *Derry Journal;* 'A star of the North-West circuit magnitude … has appeared over the hills of Dark Donegal. Mr. Denis S. Henry, Barrister, has found time in the midst of his briefs … to rush from the Derry Assizes to East Donegal to save his country.'[30] The *Derry Journal* was angry at remarks made by Henry during an election meeting held on Herdman's behalf in Letterkenny, the proceedings of which were reported in the rival Unionist newspaper, the *Londonderry Sentinel*. It seemed that when Henry rose to speak, he said that he 'desired to speak specifically to the Roman Catholic members of the audience he was addressing.'[31] It was this paragraph from the *Londonderry Sentinel*'s account which the *Derry Journal* singled out:

'While a member of another Church, he (Henry) was not afraid to stand there and say that he was not ashamed of his religion – (applause) – and that he felt, as an Irishman who had the welfare of his country at heart, he could sink religious differences and support the candidature of Mr. Herdman.'[32] Henry's use of the words 'another Church' moved the *Derry Journal* to inquire as to why he did not say 'the Catholic Church',[33] and implied that Henry was playing down his religion in order to make his presence at the meeting more acceptable to his audience. Henry's assertion that he was 'not ashamed' of his religion left the *Derry Journal* quite unimpressed: 'How satisfactory! We are absolutely appalled at the possible consequences if we were left in doubt on this point.'[34] The newspaper concluded its comments on Henry with undisguised scepticism: '… this thoughtful young man … gets away to the side of the Unionist candidate to show the people the way they should go. How poor Donegal had hitherto managed to stagger through without the helping hand of Mr. D.S. Henry is one of the marvellous things of an astonishing period.'[35]

This episode has a greater importance than one might attribute at first glance. In 1895, Henry was a barrister of rising reputation, and though sufficiently well known to have his public appearance

8

commented on by two daily newspapers, he was by no means at the peak of his profession, and could not acquire immediate political benefit from his support of a Unionist. The attitude of the Nationalists towards Henry's Unionism is also significant. The *Derry Journal*'s obvious resentment of Henry was accompanied by an open cynicism about his motives in attending Herdman's meeting. Henry is a recognised celebrity in the community – 'a rising star'; a successful barrister who is 'showered with briefs.' Yet Denis Henry is regarded as an oddity not to be taken too seriously – 'How poor Donegal has hitherto managed to stagger through without the helping hand of Mr. Henry.'

If this was typical of Ulster Nationalists, and subsequent references bear this out, then we have an indication of the kind of criticism that Henry had to contend with. Finally, the fact that the *Derry Journal* and the *Londonderry Sentinel* should devote prominent columns to Henry is an acknowledgement as to how well known a figure he was by 1895. A superficial glance over the newspaper files for July 1895 reveals why this was so. On 11 July, Henry acted before the Grand Jury of Tyrone in a case concerning an award of costs for fire damage.[36] A week later, he appeared in the Donegal Assizes,[37] while the 22, 24 and 26 July found him in Derry Assizes.[38] The travelling, time and effort involved in combining legal work with political activity attest to the demanding pace of Henry's life, which undoubtedly contributed to his sudden death in 1925.

Henry's reputation on the North-West Circuit brought recognition in 1896 when he was called to the Inner Bar.[39] On 4 June 1898, Henry became a Bencher of King's Inns.[40] Shortly afterwards, he was involved in one of the most remarkable cases of his career, for in the Winter Assizes in Belfast in December 1898, he had the unusual experience of appearing in three murder cases at a single Assize in which convictions were recorded. The Lord Chief Justice for Ireland, Sir Peter O'Brien, presided, and the Attorney General, Lord Atkinson, who led for the Crown, was assisted by Henry in each case. Three men, two from Cavan and one from Donegal, faced murder charges.

In the first case, Thomas Kelly was indicted for the murder of his father, Bernard Kelly, at Ballyconnell, Co. Cavan on 8 October 1898. Henry outlined the prosecution case: how the deceased, a popular hotel owner had an argument with his son; how several years previously the son had disappeared after a shot had been fired at his father, and how on 8 October, Thomas Kelly waited and shot his father dead. He reported the shooting to the police, yet had given no assistance to his dying father, nor had summoned either a doctor or a clergyman. The defendant was found guilty and hanged.[41] A similar sentence was carried out on Philip King, who was found guilty of murdering his mother-in-law on 30 January 1898, at Nolagh, Co. Cavan. The Attorney General revealed that the killing was part of a quadruple murder, since two of the other victims were the wife and infant child of the prisoner, while the fourth victim was a child of two years old who had died through cold and starvation. The Attorney General said that 'the case was one of the most repulsive and gruesome tragedies that ever became the lot of any jury to investigate in a court of justice.'[42] The third trial, that of Hugh Boyle of Annagry, who was accused of killing his father, Connell Boyle on 30 August 1898, deserves special mention, as it provides an example of Henry's legal ability. Shortly after a quarrel with his son over 'small and trifling things about the land,'[43] Connell Boyle died after receiving a violent blow to the head. The prosecution case was painstaking and thorough, maps of the district were used, and some witnesses were examined in Irish. The verdict of guilty, with a recommendation of mercy on account of Hugh Boyle's age, saw the accused sentenced to life imprisonment. In connection with this, Henry's summing up for the prosecution was noteworthy, for when the Lord Chief Justice addressed the jury, he remarked that Henry's speech was 'as fair a speech as was ever addressed by council representing the prosecution to a jury, because he wound up by telling them that if they wished they could disregard police evidence entirely.'[44] When passing sentence, the Lord Chief Justice commended the jury for hearing the trial with such patience, and went on; 'I think it is due to the prosecution to say that I have never heard a trial conducted on behalf of the Crown with greater fairness or in a more temperate spirit.'[45]

The 1906 general election saw Denis Henry undertake a brief of a political nature when, at the age of forty-one, he stood for the first time as a Unionist candidate for North Tyrone. This seat had been held for the Conservatives by the Hamilton family in 1885, 1886 and 1892, but the contests of 1895 and 1900 had seen C.H. Hemphill capture the seat for the Liberals.[46] The geography of North Tyrone was considered peculiar. Part of it lay right up to the Co. Derry mountains, one end of the constituency ran within four miles of Londonderry city, with the other extreme limit being the same distance from Omagh. Within these borders lay some of the richest and poorest land in Ulster.[47]

North Tyrone was no less intriguing politically, for political elements were not only intermingled, but set in groups apart. Some districts had only 3 per cent of their voters as Unionists, while in others a side-car could accommodate Nationalists for seven miles.[48] Close contests were the norm. In 1892, Hamilton's winning margin was 49 votes, while Hemphill's victories in 1895 and 1900 were by 91 and 55 votes respectively.[49] Such was the background to Denis Henry's candidature. He was to participate in a close run affair, with the narrowest winning margin in the history of North Tyrone elections determining the outcome.

The nature of the candidates involved guaranteed the North Tyrone election to be a gripping place of interest. Henry's opponent who was a Liberal, William Heuston Dodd or Sergeant Dodd, as he was professionally known, was an acquaintance of Henry at the Bar, and had been a former secretary of the Ulster Reform Association. A Protestant, and a strong supporter of the Boer War, Dodd was served by an able election agent, Dr Robert Henderson Todd, and with the anticipated allegiance of Nationalists, would be a formidable rival.[50] However, Dodd must

11

have had mixed emotions at the start of the campaign, when it was revealed that both he and James O'Connor had been passed over for the post of Solicitor-General for Ireland by Redmond Barry, who apparently was less experienced at the Bar. According to the *Northern Whig,* Barry's promotion was 'a puzzle, especially as up to the present Mr. Barry had, rightly or wrongly, the reputation of being a Unionist – that is to say, if he had any definite opinion.'[51] Dodd's endorsement at the Nationalist selection meeting in Strabane on 27 January 1906 was no foregone conclusion. Captain Hemphill, son of the retiring MP, was proposed and seconded, receiving nine votes, while the chairman, Father McHugh, PP, Strabane, had to stifle the comment that Dodd was a 'cut-and-dried' candidate.[52] The choice of the Catholic Unionist and Protestant Liberal invited much comment, and it would have been too much to expect that the main political issues should not be temporarily overlooked while the respective merits of the candidates received a rigorous examination. The *Derry Journal*, in more serious tones than before, acknowledged that Henry would be properly placed to make the most of a brief which the newspaper regarded as a desperate case.[53] It was left to the *Irish News* to strike a critical note which was maintained throughout the contest, and give an insight into the contemporary Nationalist view of Denis Henry. The newspaper regarded Henry as 'one of that weird class of creatures known as an Irish Catholic Unionist', whose 'form of disguise' would be swept away by the same kind of margin as Hemphill's in 1895.[54] The *Irish News* foresaw a dilemma for Henry; as a Unionist, he would be rejected by Catholics because of his politics, while his religion would be 'sufficient to blast his chances with the classes whose bigotry and Orangeism secure the gift of all the lucrative public positions that are going.'[55]

Nationalist disdain for Henry was matched by Unionist enthusiasm for his candidature. The *Londonderry Sentinel* readily admitted the significance of Henry being a Catholic, who could perhaps entice extra votes, and indicated that the local Unionist Association were 'quick to realise this.'[56] The *Londonderry Sentinel* saw Henry's selection as a boost for Unionism, proving that Unionist were not disruptionists, but men of conviction. Commenting on Nationalist hostility towards Henry, whose patronage of Orange halls was an obvious target, the *Londonderry Sentinel* said that Henry's support for the Orange institutions reflected his belief that the 'Orangemen of Ireland are a highly constant factor in defending the Union, and should provide themselves therefore with suitable rallying places.'[57] Henry, no novice among Unionists, had spoken for the Union in elections in North Tyrone and East Donegal, and it was confidently predicted that he would 'prosecute a vigorous campaign against Dodd.'[58]

Henry lost no time in making clear his attitude to the main issues of the day, and he outlined his views on the Union:

> I am opposed to the establishment of any separate Legislature for this country, or to any Legislature which may in any way tend to weaken the Union between this country and the rest of the United Kingdom. Whether this change is sought to be effected by a Home Rule Bill, or under the guise of Devolution, it shall have my strongest opposition.[59]

Dodd's election address gave similar prominence to the Union, and contained a 'frank and distinct declaration on the fullest question of the fullest measure of self-government for Ireland, consistent with the supremacy of Parliament and the integrity of the United Kingdom.'[60] The *Londonderry Sentinel* was concerned that a Liberal victory would give Home Rulers the opportunity to present Dodd as indicating the majority political view of Presbyterians in Ireland. It made the consequence of Unionist defeat in North Tyrone more serious – regardless of how the other contests were going throughout the country.[61]

In his campaign speeches, Henry elaborated his views on the Union. At Strabane, on 5 January 1906, he said that it was the finality of Home Rule which made the measure particularly dangerous, and he warned his audience that a Home Rule Act could not be repealed or amended, since sole representation would be in Dublin.[62] At a meeting in Castlederg that same day, Henry said that Ireland was free enough, since existing constitutional arrangements ensured that there was no religion in Ireland subsidised by the government at the expense of any other, and men were free to do as they wished, without injuring their fellow countrymen.[63] At Plumbridge, on 8 January, Henry used the 'distinctiveness of Ulster' argument against Home Rule, namely, that a Home Rule government would have little sympathy with Ulster or its industries. He could see little in common with the rest of Ireland, saying that the south, east and west represented 'quite a different community altogether.'[64] This speech seems to represent a hardening of Henry's Unionism. In Letterkenny in 1895, he had spoken to Unionists as an 'Irishman.' Now, in 1906, he appeared before them in Tyrone as an Ulsterman, highlighting all those things that were beneficial to Ulster under the Union. Undoubtedly, maintenance of the Union was Henry's watchword, so much so that in Strabane he offered to withdraw from the contest if his opponent would reject Home Rule 'in any shape or form.'[65]

The 1906 election also revealed Henry's attitude towards education, the welfare of the agricultural community and fiscal reform. Perhaps drawing on his own experiences in Dundalk, Chesterfield and Queen's College, Henry endorsed the establishment of a university for separate all denominations in Ireland, stating that it was 'essential to the future well being of this country that students of all religions should associate together during their university career.'[66] On agriculture, Henry pledged support for the provision of 'decent and comfortable dwellings' for labourers,[67] and advocated legislation to increase the facilities given to occupying tenants for their purchase of their holdings by agreement. Henry's support of compulsory purchase urged Lord Frederick Hamilton to declare that Denis Henry was the first Unionist representative to uphold a measure for the sale of Irish land which went even beyond the Wyndham Act.[68] The *Derry Journal*, however, remained unmoved, and said that Henry had never done anything for tenants or land reform, and queried when he had ever conceded land purchase important.[69]

Fiscal reform, and the adverse effects of foreign competition on Irish agriculture, received much attention in the campaign speeches. At Castlederg, on 5 January 1906, Henry's comments on falling prices among agricultural products encouraged one spectator to bemoan the fact that beef was only costing '4d per pound', whereupon Henry replied that the system of free trade was to blame.[70] At the same meeting, H.T. Barrie, who assisted Henry throughout, said that a ton of potatoes sent to America was 38/6d., which was more than the price of a ton of potatoes in this country.[71] Henry promised to support legislation to lessen undue foreign competition, 'and secure for the farmer better prices, for the artisan and labourer better wages.' Both candidates indicated consensus in opposing the removal of restrictions on the importation of Canadian and foreign cattle, believing that the opening of Irish ports to such cattle would destroy the Irish farmers' principal market for young stock.[72] Curiously enough, the *Londonderry Sentinel* believed that the outcome of the election could hinge on the fiscal question, seeing Dodd's reluctance to countenance restrictions on foreign meat imported from America, which in the *Sentinel*'s view was the real cause of low prices in Ireland, as a glaring weakness in his programme.[73]

A talking point throughout the North Tyrone election was the relationship between Denis Henry, local Unionists and the Orange Order. Walter Long, MP, endorsed Henry's candidature with these words: 'I know of nobody better qualified than you to take a leading part in Parliament, and I heartily wish you every success.'[74] Joseph Chamberlain, in a letter to Henry, wrote that the contest was 'a critical one for the loyal minority in Ireland, whose rights and interests are again threatened by a combination between the Radicals and Nationalists.'[75] Meetings of Orangemen in Killeter, Leckpatrick and Strabane passed encouraging resolutions in this vein:

...we pledge ourselves to support Mr. Denis Stanislaus Henry, KC, the Unionist candidate for North Tyrone, at the forthcoming election, and earnestly call upon our brethren to do all in their power to receive his return.[76]

This kind of association with Protestants in general and Orangemen in particular aroused a mixture of indignation and bemusement among Nationalists. Mr P. Lafferty, JP, who chaired Dodd's opening election meeting in Newtownstewart, confessed that the contest was unique in the history of Ulster, in that for the *first time* the Unionist banner at a parliamentary election was being carried by a Roman Catholic, while the 'popular cause' was upheld by a Presbyterian.[77] The Rev. Philip O'Doherty, PP, speaking with some bewilderment at 'this incredible state of affairs' in North Tyrone, commented that while Justice Kenny had merely been a Catholic Unionist, Denis Henry had embraced the Orange faction too. Father O'Doherty told his audience of 3,000 that as a 'close student' of Irish history, he believed 'that in the records of Irish electoral contests it was a thing unknown to have a Catholic supported by the Orange lodges.'[78] Henry's supporters at Drumquin were told by J.R. Patchill, KC, that their candidate represented 'a curious difference to probably every other candidate who had sought their votes.'[79] The *Derry Journal* opened its columns to those who wished to convey their distaste of Henry's candidature in a more poetic form. To 'Brother Dinish' was thus addressed these lines:

A Papist beating the Orange Drum!
Surely no slavery could be 'maner?'
To what base uses you have come
In the hope of a North Tyrone retainer![80]

A more serious response to Denis Henry came from a correspondent in the *Derry Journal* whose letter, predicting that Orange support for Henry and Orange votes were two distinct things, caused some agitation among Unionists.[81] This opinion prompted a hasty rebuke from a Unionist who wrote to the *Londonderry Sentinel* denying the existence of any

16

compulsion upon Orangemen to vote for Protestant nominees only. The writer claimed that a candidate was merely asked for an affirmative answer to the following question, which, when given, made him acceptable:

> Do you promise to avoid and discountenance all societies and associations composed of persons who seek to subvert the just prerogative of the Crown, the independence of each branch of the Legislature, the established rights of property, and the Union which connects these Kingdoms?[82]

Considering the circumstances, this keenly fought election was surprisingly free of ill-feeling. It was conducted at a daunting pace, with the candidates addressing several different meetings in one day. The personalities of the candidates contributed to good conduct, and the mutual respect between Henry and Dodd was never in any doubt. The only lapse in discipline among spectators came when Dodd's election meeting at Bready was attacked, by what the *Derry Journal* alleged was an 'Orange gang', engaged in 'ear-splitting outbreaks of organised obstruction.'[83] Henry found time to demonstrate his humour on Dodd's supporters, informing Ignatius O'Brien, KC, that Dodd would make a good deal out of Home Rule – especially as a bankruptcy lawyer.[84] To Dr Wylie, Henry attributed the unenviable distinction of having made only one important speech before – and that was when he thanked the Sheriff for reminding him he was bottom of the poll.[85]

The poll was taken on 19 January 1906, and the result was as follows:

> W.H.Dodd (L) 2, 966
> D.S.Henry (U) 2, 957

The margin was 9 votes, extremely close, 'not so wide as a church door or as deep as a draw well,' but enough to see Dodd home safely.[86]

The day's proceedings opened soberly, livened considerably, and induced a feeling of climax which the final count did nothing to dissolve. According to the *Londonderry Sentinel*, 96.4 % of

Unionists cast their votes, and out of a total electorate of 6,174, there were 5,954 votes registered, an outstanding tribute to the organisational flair, and perhaps the personating ability of both sides.[87] Nearly two of the five hours spent on counting were occupied with argument over an amazing lapse of error by the presiding officer, E.M. Archdale. It transpired that when Archdale accounted for the Drumquin box, he did not mark the voters' registration number of the ballot paper counterfoil to show the vote cast, but mistakengly marked it on the back of the ballot paper, making it possible to undermine the secrecy of the ballot by reference to the register. This occurred in 48 cases, and it was alleged that many of these votes had been cast for Dodd.[88] William Wilson, Henry's campaign agent, argued that these 48 ballot papers should be considered as spoiled. Dr Todd, on behalf of W.H. Dodd, said that since the voters themselves had not marked the numbers then they should not be deprived of the vote.[89] The *Derry Journal* reported Denis Henry's role in this debate: 'Mr. Henry ... was vigorously hissed by the crowd...smoking a cigar, Mr Henry appeared. He was vigorously hissed by the crowd. In reply to our representative, he stated that he did not desire a recount of the vote, and that the figures already announced might be regarded as definite.'[90] On an occasion which must have assuaged so much disappointment, Henry exchanged greetings with Dodd, offered his congratulations, praised Dodd's professional ability, and promised to continue to be his friend. The election, Henry told a gathering afterwards, had shown that the North of Ireland was as tolerant as anywhere else in the United Kingdom; 'although we are technically beaten for the time being ... we have secured a splendid moral victory.'[91]

This attitude of Henry, while giving us an insight into his personality, still raises the question as to why, after committing himself to a cause which meant so much to him, he did not appeal against the controversial result of the election. The *Irish News* outlined the options available. Under existing electoral law, a defeated candidate with a grievance could present a petition to the High Court. There, he could demand a recount, a scrutiny, or a combination of both. When a petition was presented, the petitioner would check the ballot papers of the successful candidate, and the scrutiny (an inquiry into the validity of each vote appearing on each party's list of voters objected to), would take place at the trial, after the recriminating case had been made.[92]

Denis Henry had no part of this procedure. If he had appealed, and the result reversed, he would have entered parliament in 1906 instead of 1916. One wonders how satisfying such a victory would have been for Henry: a Catholic, representing Unionists, aided by Orangemen and assisted by legal technicalities? The complete truth of this will never be known, but perhaps Henry wanted to reach parliament strictly on his own merits, without dispute, just as he had done in his professional life. Conversely, an unsuccessful appeal could have reflected badly on Henry, and could have left him open to the charge that he was desperate for political advancement. Instead, Henry accepted defeat, and withdrew. With the Liberal majority falling from 55 to 9 votes, North Tyrone was by no means overwhelmingly for Home Rule. Two clues have merged to Henry's thinking on this episode. One, a brief letter to an unknown recipient on 17 February, is worth quoting in full:

Sir,

Allow me to thank you heartily for your support during the late Election. I am greatly indebted to you for your vote and efforts on my behalf. May I ask another favour from you. Give any help you can towards the Revision. Every vote is needed, and if you know of a man who can possibly get a vote, let the Inspector for your District know at once. Again thanking you cordially.

I remain,
your obedient servant,

DENIS S. HENRY

28, Fitzwilliam Square, Dublin.[93]

19

Reference to the Revision Court conveys a hint of frustration at a possible cause of the 9 vote defeat, while the exhortation to locate extra votes suggests Henry's determination to enter parliament very soon. At the age of forty-one, he might have felt that time was not on his side. That being the case, the manner with which he accepted his defeat is more noteworthy. Henry was more forthcoming in a speech made at Strabane on 6 March 1907, when, in reference to his election defeat by a technicality, he said that he had declined to use a petition, although advised by leaders of the Bar that a petition would be successful, 'because he felt that sooner or later an opportunity would be given to the Unionists in North Tyrone to again fight out the battle.'[94]

If the North Tyrone election proved that it was possible for a Catholic to win Protestant votes, it also revealed that little cross-voting took place. The *Londonderry Sentinel* investigated the poll on a religious basis, and produced these figures:

Total number of Roman Catholics voting: 2,986.
Total number of votes for Dodd 2,966.
Total number of Protestants voting: 2,964.
Total number of votes for Henry: 2,957.[95]

The newspaper concluded that Henry received, broadly speaking, a Roman Catholic vote for every Protestant vote given to Dodd.[96] It appears that voting took place on strictly party lines, and that Henry did not win over a sizeable percentage of the Nationalist vote. In conclusion, Henry lost no credibility with Unionists over this defeat, and the *Londonderry Sentinel*'s verdict was that no Unionist candidate could possibly have done more: 'All honour to the popular and eloquent Unionist candidate who thus rallied such a splendid following to the standard he so pluckily and so honourably held aloft.'[97]

A year after the North Tyrone contest of 1906, W.H. Dodd became a Judge, and there was a vacancy in the constituency in February 1907.[98] The Liberal government was now well established, and there was much speculation about imminent proposals for Irish self-government (eventually embodied in the ill-fated Irish Council Bill later that year), and with this in mind, the Liberals, Nationalists and Unionists were keen to utilise North Tyrone as a gauge of opinion in Ireland. For Denis Henry, it was a welcome opportunity to bring the situation back to parity, and repay the faith of his Unionist colleagues by delivering the seat. At first glance, the occasion of another election in the same constituency within the space of thirteen months might imply a subdued affair, yet the reality was different. Everyone in the constituency, not least the candidates themselves, worked to make the North Tyrone by-election of 1907 'one of the most stubbornly fought election contests in the annals of modern electioneering.'[99]

If the Unionists were quick to declare their candidate – it was reported that within one hour of the vacancy being announced circulars were sent to outvoters[100] – then the Liberals and Nationalists required more time for deliberation. The attributes of Sir William F. Butler, of Bansha Castle, Tipperary, made him a popular option with the *Irish News*, but on 2 March 1907, Redmond Barry was chosen as Henry's opponent. A fellow KC and colleague at the Bar, Barry was a native of County Cork, and had been Solicitor-General for Ireland since 1905.[101] Like Dodd before him, Barry had the backing of the Nationalists.

The candidates announced, the Nationalists lost no time in predicting a successful outcome, and their criticisms of Henry became more scathing. Protestant Nationalists, it was said, took the side of Ireland because of patriotism, but the 'Orange-Catholic gentleman' from Draperstown was accused of seeking a 'place and lucre'[102] in the ranks of his country's enemies; 'Protestant Nationalists are men of honour, and conscience, and conviction; find us a Catholic Unionist who is not, in some posture or another, a whipper at the shrine of the golden calf.'[103] Not only was Denis Henry considered a curiosity of the political scene in Ulster, but he was now seen as a traitor to his country, a self-seeker and an opportunist. One writer contrived a bizarre argument, claiming that Henry must have thanked his lucky stars that he had not succeeded in 1906, for he had 'escaped the penalised privilege of attending Parliament in hopeless shade of opposition for the term of five years or seven as the case may be.'[104]

Amidst the predictable arguments over Home Rule, the election raised other new points. If Henry was a self-seeker, he certainly did not display much gratitude at having the chance to rectify the result, for the subject of Dodd's elevation to the Judgeship was much criticised. Henry said that the Labourers' Act of 1906 was to be partly financed from two Judgeships, which were to be abolished, along with a reduction in the salary of the Lord Chancellor. But the appointment of Dodd had put an end to that scheme: his £3,500 a year salary could have built 500 labourers' cottages.[105] Henry's meeting in Drumquin on 28 February 1907 was interrupted by a Nationalist who claimed that the overcrowded Land Courts in Dublin justified the attention of another judge like Dodd. Henry replied that when the Conservatives decided not to fill the vacancy, which arose during their term of office, there were 15,000 land cases to be dealt with, of which 9,000 had been disposed without the assistance of another Judge.[106] In a meeting at Strabane on 2 March, Redmond Barry revealed that the government had yielded to representations from the Irish Party to appoint a second Judge to do the work of the Land Commission.[107] He added that over £4 million had been allocated for the financing of the Labourers' Act, and not a penny would be withdrawn. He accused Henry of 'running a mischievous and blighting religious cry.'[108]

The 1907 by-election provided more evidence of the support that Henry enjoyed from Unionists, contrary to Nationalist speculation. H.T.Barrie, J. Gordon, KC and P.C. Gausen all spoke during Henry's meetings, and on 1 March 1907, the Ulster Liberal Unionist Association passed the following resolution at their Belfast meeting:

> The winning of North Tyrone at the present juncture, when a Home Rule Government for the third time proposes to throw the Constitution of Ireland into the melting pot, and to destroy

that security which is the basis of individual, commercial and agricultural prosperity of the province, would be an event of the utmost importance to the cause of the Union, and would materially strengthen the hands of the Unionist Party in Parliament.'[109]

The anticipated close result promoted a multitude of forecasts about the voters' intentions. It was a great source of speculation as to whether the Presbyterians would vote for Henry or Barry – or even abstain. Dr Todd, in whose experienced hands Barry's campaign was entrusted, was only prepared to reveal names on two of the thirteen nomination papers because, he said, Presbyterian supporters of Barry 'might be subject to annoyance' if the names were published, 'as happened before.'[110] T.W. Russell claimed that Barry's candidature was 'quite hopeless', as Nationalists would not go with him, and discounted the 'invisible army of Protestant Home Rulers' in Barry's favour.[111] The *Daily Mail* reporter in the constituency declared that Barry was pursuing a double-barrelled campaign: his rousing of the Nationalist vote risked splitting the Presbyterian vote or even inducing an appreciable percentage of Presbyterians to abstain.[112] An interesting twist in the campaign was a letter from 'A Good Orangeman', who wrote that he would vote for neither Henry or Barry, and quoted one of the principal rules of the Orange Society by way of explanation:

…it is…required of you that should you now be in possession of the electoral franchise you will support by your vote and interest Orange and Protestant candidates only…Your neglecting to fulfil these conditions will render you liable to expulsion.[113]

If Denis Henry could expect trouble from Orangemen, then the *Londonderry Sentinel* warned that Nationalists might be lukewarm about Barry, who was unpledged, 'and some (Nationalists) may come to the conclusion that as long as they are content to vote for an unpledged candidate so long will they be asked to do so, and may resolve to withhold their support.'[114] The newspaper printed a letter from a correspondent who said that Nationalists would oppose, in principle, the 'Whig or Tory lawyer', and went on: 'there are many real Nationalists in North Tyrone who will cut off their right hand sooner than put a cross opposite the name of a British government Solicitor-General.' The writer signed himself 'Sinn Fein.'[115]

At the beginning of the election, Henry had promised Barry 'a merry good humoured fight but with a determined effort to place that gentleman at the bottom of the poll.'[116] He was true to his word. Each side worked tirelessly, with the candidates at times holding several meetings in a single day,[117] while in a five-day period Henry conducted twelve meetings in different parts of the county.[118] It is to Henry's credit that, amidst his comments about the importance of the occasion, and his frank admission of physical fatigue, he should remind his audiences to conduct themselves properly, saying that he would tolerate no disorder.[119] Only one indiscretion marred the proceedings when, at Ardstraw, eggs were thrown at Barry's supporters. A Mr Crae caught one egg, unbroken, in the palm of his hand, and had a souvenir, as well as his only talking point, thereafter. The Rev. Bradley, a Presbyterian minister, was less fortunate, and caught his egg more conventionally on the back of his neck.[120] Henry himself was involved in an amusing incident, though he was a reluctant participant. A traction-engine had broken down midway between Claudy and Glentimon, and blocked the road preventing Henry's wagonette from passing. Henry alighted and decided to walk, as he had a meeting to address. When a passing car offered him a lift, Henry laughingly declined, saying that his destination was only a quarter of a mile further on. In fact, the meeting was two miles away. Henry's arrival, forty-five minutes late, was reported by the *Irish News*; 'It will not be a surprise to learn that the speech which the candidate subsequently delivered was remarkable for its brevity.'[121]

The poll took place on 9 March 1907, and testified to the efforts of the respective parties to capture the seat. It was said that a more exhaustive poll had never been made anywhere, with over 99% of each candidate's followers turning out.[122] The remarkably high poll is easier to understand when one examines the work of the parties on polling day. Denis Henry had an impressive array of vehicles, and twenty-four motor cars.[123] Barryite and Henryite supporters positioned petrol and repair stations at a number of points and had breakdown gangs ready.[124] Plumbridge, where only two votes were unaccounted for in 1906, had a perfect system: they all polled together in Newtownstewart, and those with cars brought those who had not.[125] The aged, infirm and disabled participated too. At Newtownstewart, brandy was administered to one man who was grateful to live long enough to vote for Denis Henry.[126] A blind man who asked the presiding officer to mark for Henry was objected to by Nationalists, and the argument lasted a full hour before he could proceed.[127] Two Nationalists died on their way to the poll – one in the arms of friends while he was being lifted out of bed. Almost all the Unionists outvoters came to vote. Mr W. Sinclair arrived from Buenos Aires to vote for Denis Henry (he had been on his way to a Mediterranean holiday, but clearly deemed North Tyrone more important).[128] Catholic priests stood outside polling booths and supported Barry, as did Sinn Feiners and members of the AOH. One man who had not been to the polls for fifteen years voted for Henry.

The result of the 1907 North Tyrone by-election was:

R. Barry: (L) 3,013
D. Henry: (U) 3,006

Barry won by a margin of 7 votes. (In 1906, the Liberals had won North Westmoreland by 3 votes, while Joseph Devlin's West Belfast victory in the same year had been by 16 votes.)

Once again Henry was defeated by the closest winning margin in the history of North Tyrone. Speaking at the Abercorn Arms hotel after the result, Henry's words reinforced the character he had displayed in coming to terms with his bitter disappointment the previous year:

> I was glad to come and fight your battle, and I have been manfully supported…none of you should allow himself to be carried away

in the heat of this election into acts of violence..if you keep the peace you will please me as much as if you had returned me[129]

The Unionist newspapers commiserated with Henry . The *Londonderry Sentinel* was saddened not only by the loss of the seat, but by the loss to the Unionists in parliament of someone of Henry's calibre.[130] The *Northern Whig* said that Henry had been a 'model candidate', and hoped 'that before long some Ulster constituency will be fortunate enough to secure his services'.[131] The *Irish Times* admitted candid disappointment at the result,[132] while the *Daily Express* observed that the electorate in Great Britain needed education on the Irish problem, 'and if Mr. Denis Henry's defeat leads to greater political activity in this quarter there is the prospect that out of a political reverse political good may come.'[133]

The voting figures were examined by the *Derry Journal*, the *Londonderry Sentinel*, the *Times* and the *Irish News*. W.T. Miller, secretary of the North Tyrone Unionist Association, claimed that Barry had obtained the exact number of Catholic votes that were polled, i.e. 3,013. He maintained that thirty-six Protestants had abstained,[134] though the *Derry Journal* put that figure nearer twenty-six.[135] The *Derry Journal*'s opinion was that seventy Protestants and Presbyterians had voted for Barry,[136] while a letter in the *Londonderry Sentinel* reckoned this number to be between forty and fifty.[137] Whatever the analysis, nothing could alter the fact that Denis Henry, KC, had failed to reach the goal that many Ulster Unionists felt he deserved.

Denis Henry had little respite after the exertions of North Tyrone. A few days after the poll, a vacancy in North Belfast arose when the Unionist, Daniel Dixon, died. The Nationalist press immediately linked Henry with a possible nomination, claiming that Henry was visiting Belfast to secure the candidature.[138] While the validity of the claim is uncertain, it is known that Henry busied himself professionally, attending the Co. Tyrone Crown Court on 11 March, the following day the Record Court, and the Omagh Crown Court on the 13 March.

On 23 March 1907, it was reported that the General Committee of the Conservative Association met in Clifton Street Orange Hall, and selected G. S. Clark, of Workman and Clark Ltd, to oppose the Labour man, William Walker, in North Belfast.[139] Although the speculation about Henry proved misplaced, it did not prevent the *Irish News* from questioning Henry's future relationship with the Unionist Party. The newspaper said that having a Catholic Unionist in North Tyrone was a less distasteful thing than 'bringing a Papist right into the heart of the fold in the big "home farm" of Belfast.'[140] The *Irish News* ventured that Henry was about to share the fate of one Michael J.F. McCarthy – presumably another Catholic Unionist – who was welcomed on 'Old Order' platforms until he developed the impudence enough to claim the Tory nomination for South Dublin, whereupon he disappeared from the political scene.[141] Retrospectively, this was a valid conclusion to come to. Henry had fought for the Unionists in a determined manner, yet lost each time. Moreover, the defeats were only fourteen months apart, in the same constituency, where the business of electioneering was practised to a fine art, and taken very seriously. However tight the margins, it would have been understandable if Unionists had lost patience with their Catholic ally. Yet things did not quite work out that way. An idea of the attitude of Unionists towards Henry was given by Sir James Henry when he revealed a silver tray, which bore the following inscription:

This Service of Plate
Was Presented to
DENIS S. HENRY, KC
By the Unionist women of North Tyrone
In Recognition of His Two Spirited Contests
In That Constituency
1906-1907

Parliament and promotion
1907–1919

IN OCTOBER 1910, Denis Henry married Violet Holmes, the third daughter of Lord Justice Holmes.[1] In a sense it was thought to be a strange union, with Denis and his wife coming from different social backgrounds, and Violet being a member of the Church of Ireland. In another sense, the marriage was no surprise, since Denis Henry had been acquainted with the Holmes family, and Violet in particular, for years.[2] Henry was forty-six, his wife was thirty-two. They had five children; James, born in 1911, Denise, Alice, Denis and Lorna. The children were reared as Catholics, while Violet resisted all attempts to convert her to the Catholic faith. It was a very happy marriage, but was quite short-lived, lasting only fifteen years.[3]

The disappointments of North Tyrone set aside, Denis Henry threw himself into his legal work, and by 1914 had established the reputation of being one of the most outstanding advocates in Ireland. He worked extensively in the North-West Circuit, becoming the Father, while newspaper files reveal his name appearing regularly in Dublin court cases where he had a successful practice at the Four Courts. Between 1911 and 1914, it is interesting to note that when Nationalists pressed their claims at the Registration courts, Henry regularly represented the Unionists, where claims and counter-claims were keenly disputed.[4] Some material signs indicate Henry's success, for in his will of 30 November 1910, Henry was able to bequeath to his trustees, William Gage and Patrick J. Henry, the sum of £16,000, the income arriving from this to be paid to his wife. By an undated codicil he reduced this figure to £14,000, appointing his brothers Patrick and Alexander to be his trustees.[5] However, Henry still found time to support the Unionist cause on several occasions during the Home Rule crisis of 1912-1914. Speaking in Dublin in November 1912, Henry argued that a Home Rule parliament would do little to protect the rights of minorities, and pointed out that in 'the thirty years' since he had come to Dublin, no Unionist had held public office under the corporation. If Home Rule were passed, he said, the loyal minority would be subject to a combination of 'metropolitan misfits and provincial pirates.'[6] Henry made no attempt to contest North Tyrone – or any other seat – in the general elections of January and December 1910. In late 1909, it was reported that 'Mr. Denis Henry, KC ... is unable to permit himself to be nominated (for North Tyrone) owing to increasing professional duties'.[7] Not only was Henry absent from the campaign, where Emmerson Crawford Herdman, nephew of his old friend E.T. Herdman, stood against the incumbent, Redmond Barry, but Henry was one of those whose names were listed under the heading 'apologies for inability to attend' regarding the annual meeting of the Ulster Unionist Council in Belfast on 4 January 1910.[8]

The lack of private papers on Henry's legal work is partially assuaged by the amount of available contemporary records which testify both to his qualities as a lawyer and his personal attributes. William Evelyn Wylie, later to become a Law Adviser to the Crown when Henry was Attorney-General during the Anglo-Irish war, provides vivid recollections of Henry at the Bar. In an unpublished memo, written sometime between 1939 and 1951, Wylie recalled how nervous he used to be when he obtained a brief: 'I nearly died of sheer nerves. I never slept if I had a case the next day and used to feel as sick as a dog before I got up in Court.' However, Wylie must have been assured by Henry's remark that he felt much the same, confiding, 'I never go down to the Courts after a long vacation without wondering have I been found out or could I be found out this term.' Then he said, 'you'll always be nervous, and you wouldn't be worth a damn if you weren't.'

For Wylie, Henry was 'the quickest thinker and most brilliant advocate' that he ever knew; 'To the last day when I was against him I always felt like a small terrier dog after a bicycle. You thought you had him and away he would go on a new point and have the case won before you knew what was happening. Before a weak judge he was invincible and to put up even a decent show you had to get onto your toes and stay there all the time'. Ironically, the only Judge with whom Henry failed to 'cut no more ice before him than did a Junior' was Lord Justice Holmes.[9]

Insights such as these on Henry also reveal something of the atmosphere and camaraderie in the Irish Bar in the late nineteenth and early twentieth century. T.J. Campbell records how in the Law Library in the Four Courts, 'witticisms flashed swift and bright as swords at play.' He remarked that 'To listen in the circle often formed around Tim Healy or Denis Henry … was to enjoy a feast of reason …The Library was a microcosm of the life of Ireland … political foes sat cheek by jowl … good companions all.'[10] Campbell said that Denis Henry was 'among the wittiest and readiest raconteurs in the Law Library',[11] and recalled the occasion when William Johnson, who was nicknamed 'Wooden-headed Billy' appeared in court with his head bandaged, and explained, 'nothing serious. Just a splinter under my finger nail'. 'He must have been scratching his head', murmured Henry to Tim Healy.[12] Wylie regarded the old North-West Circuit as a 'wonderful institution', and wrote, 'Poor old Denis. What do we of the old North-West Circuit not owe him.' Wylie described how the tradition arose on this Circuit that all at the Bar were expected to dine together unless the Father gave leave of absence, and went on, 'Every shade of politics, religion and lack of religion was represented on the Circuit yet I never heard a bitter word said.' As Denis once said, 'If 20 doctors were travelling round together as we are, they would all be dead before they started or shortly afterwards.' There was little jealousy over briefs, 'and the chat after dinner with Denis as Father and John Patchell as Chief Assistant will never be equalled in Ireland again.'[13] Alexander Martin Sullivan, who as Sergeant Sullivan defended Roger Casement in 1916, wrote that Denis Henry had been 'the best man that the Irish Bar produced in my time. He had a clear deep mind comparable to that of the Lord Chief Baron Palles. His features were handsome, his carriage dignified, and he was meant, with his splendid genius and delightful humour, to be the leader of his profession.'[14] Henry's ability to mix and socialise with legal contemporaries was facilitated by his association with a wide network of clubs, the membership of which he shared with other legal men no less well known than himself. Henry joined the Constitutional Club and University Dublin along with D.M. Wilson (Solicitor-General for Ireland 1919–1921) and A.W. Samuels (Attorney-General for Ireland in 1918). Like Wilson, Henry was also a member of the Ulster Club, Belfast, and the Royal Ulster Yacht Club, and shared membership of the Carlton Club with Samuels.[15]

One of Denis Henry's most publicised cases in the pre-war era came in January 1914 when, along with S.L. Brown, KC, he was chosen to head a Commission of Inquiry into the circumstances of the famous riots which followed the Larkinite demonstration in Dublin in August 1913.[16] During a disturbance lasting only several minutes, two people died, 400 were injured, and scores of police wielded batons to control the crowds.[17] The choice of Brown and Henry was welcomed by the *Irish Law Times and Solicitors' Journal,* which commented that 'for such an inquiry, no better selection could be made. They combine great ability and high standing at the Bar, with a judicial temper admirably adapted for the duties they have undertaken.'[18]

The inquiry sat from 6 to 29 January 1914, and the Commissioners heard conflicting accounts of the riots from policemen, representatives of Dublin Corporation, and members of the public. Emotions ran high at times, and Handle Booth's heated exchanges with the police legal representative, Mr Powell, were treated firmly but quietly by Henry, who was economical in his use of words throughout, and always kept to the point at hand.[19] The Report issued by Henry and Brown in February 1914 contained a large measure of exoneration for the police. One paragraph referred to the violence which occurred after meetings and (which witnessed) much 'inflammatory language', and went on: 'In their efforts to cope with the rioters the police were obliged in every case to draw their batons and disperse with force stone-throwing crowds.' As a result, over 30 policemen were hurt, many of whom were unfit for duty for several weeks. The Report found that the police procedures for controlling the crowd were 'wise and ineffectual.' The police were cleared of charges of brutality, though some members were found to have committed unjustifiable assaults, and of deliberately damaging several Corporation buildings.[20]

In the early years of the war, Henry temporarily set aside his professional activities and once again attempted to secure a Westminster seat. This opportunity for Henry to redress the disappointments of North Tyrone came in April 1916, when Justice Gordon was elevated to a judgeship, thereby creating a vacancy in the South Derry constituency.[21] The South Derry Unionist Association nominated Henry to succeed Gordon, a decision welcomed by the *Londonderry Sentinel,* which reminded its readers that the wartime political truce between Nationalists, Liberals and Unionists would make Henry's unopposed return 'practically certain'.[22] The newspaper failed to reveal, however, that Denis Henry was by no means a unanimous choice as the Unionist candidate, and that the behind-the-scenes activity to secure the nomination would in fact be far more difficult than the actual contest itself. It appears that when the South Derry Unionist Association met on 22 April, Lieutenant-Colonel Chichester, D.D. Reid and Denis Henry presented themselves as possible candidates, and it required three ballots by the delegates before a decision was reached. Reid appeared to have much in common with Henry. Educated at Queen's College, he entered the English Bar, opened chambers at Lincoln's Inn, and lost the East Tyrone election of December 1910 by 140 votes to W.A. Redmond. After the first ballot, Reid, Henry and Chichester received 9 votes apiece from the South Derry delegates. In the second ballot, Chichester, Henry and Reid received 10, 9 and 8 votes respectively. Before the final vote, Reid withdrew, and in a straight fight with Chichester, Henry came out on top by 17 votes to 10, apparently benefiting from the Reid vote.[23] Whether these proceedings betray Unionist doubts about Henry, or reflect genuine regard for three potentially good candidates, is uncertain. Henry had, after all, fought and lost twice in North Tyrone, the last occasion being nine years before, and in the intervening period had devoted most of his time to his legal work. Whatever the reasoning behind the delegates' voting, there was no inevitability about Henry's nomination.

Within hours of the nomination day, the *Derry Journal* broke the surprising news that Henry would, after all, have to contest the seat. His opponent was a Dr Arthur Turnball, from Glasgow. A lieutenant in the Royal Army Medical Corps, Turnball described himself as a 'National Union Covenant' candidate, independent of party ties and contemptuous of party truces.[24] Turnball opposed conscription for Ireland 'without the verdict of the Irish people', and wanted to see a 'more vigorous prosecution' of the war by a freely elected House of Commons.[25] Dr. Turnball's commitment to the war effort can be gauged from the fact that several weeks before, in the House of Commons, he leapt from the Strangers' Gallery onto the floor of the House, to insist on the provision of steel helmets for soldiers at the front.[26] However, the electoral history of the constituency was in Henry's favour, as traditionally South Derry returned Unionists, with Thomas Lea and John Gordon KC being the sitting members from 1886–1900 and 1900–1916 respectively. With the exception of 1900, when Gordon was returned unopposed, Unionists had always faced a fight for the seat, with the main challenge coming from the Liberals. The last time the Nationalists had contested South Derry was in 1886, when Tim Healy lost to Lea by 106 votes in a poll of 9366. Close contests were quite common. In 1906, Gordon defeated the Liberal, Keightley, by 71 votes, overcame the same opponent in January 1910 by 307 votes, and beat W. J. Johnston in December that year by 332 votes.[27] Henry's candidature would have a more straightforward outcome.

Even though Turnball was an independent candidate, his very presence in the field proved a source of embarrassment to Henry's opponents and annoyance to Henry's supporters. The South Derry Nationalist and Liberal Association met in Magherafelt and disowned Turnball,[28] while in an election meeting in Kilrea, on 17 May 1916, Denis Henry read a letter from the Ulster Liberal Unionist Association saying that Turnball's candidature was without their knowledge or support.[29] At the same meeting, Henry dismissed his opponent's programme as 'ludicrous', and regretted the fact that the truce had not been observed.[30] An editorial in the *Northern Whig* referred to the 'wholly superfluous election', and praised Henry as someone who 'both on political and personal grounds ... is fully worthy of all the support he can possibly receive'. The political background to the election was not lost on the *Northern Whig,* which reminded its readers that South Derry was 'the first contested election in Ulster since the Nationalist rebellion and since Mr. Dillon...declared in the Commons that he was "proud" of the rebels.' In these circumstances, a vote for Henry was seen as a vote for Unionism, and in the 'present critical state, it would be little less than treason to the cause they have at heart' to abstain.[31]

Subsequent events did little to dispel the expectation that if Turnball had succeeded in reaching the floor of the Commons by less conventional means, he would have little chance of doing so by the more traditional process of an election win. At all his meetings, Turnball was greeted with an unfriendly atmosphere, as he faced audiences whom he had never met before and who were confident that he would never be seen again. A mainly Unionist crowd attended a Turnball meeting at Moneymore on 18 May, whereupon Turnball's description of himself as a 'Scotchman, with an Irish grandmother', was met with the reply, 'A good Scotchman has no call to come here'. When challenged about the party truce, Turnball said, 'I don't consider any contract or party truce where life is concerned'. To a chorus of 'Three cheers for Denis Henry,' the meeting concluded, with Turnball leaving amidst loud jeering.[32] At Maghera, L. R. Hastings, solicitor for Turnball, said that his candidate wished no man to support him unless he wanted to. This scarcely decisive comment was followed by Turnball's refusal to be drawn on the Home Rule question, and the meeting ended in uproar.[33] In a rare election meeting, Henry told an audience in Magherafelt that it was thirty-one years since he had appeared in the town with the first case he ever had. There was a unanimous vote of support from the 'Loyalist electors of the Magherafelt polling district.'[34] The brief campaign provided more evidence of Unionist warmth for Henry. The half-yearly meeting of County Tyrone Orange Lodge in Dungannon on 19 May, 'mindful of the gallant fight put up at two elections in this county', wished Henry all success, and expressed confidence that 'the brethren in (South Derry) will give him whole-hearted support.'[35] Col. Chichester chaired Henry's final meeting in Castledawson Protestant Hall, and expressed confidence that the Orangemen and Protestants of South Derry would show the rest of the country that they were free from bigotry, and would rally to the support of a Catholic Unionist as loyally as to a Protestant.[36]

The proceedings on polling day, 23 May 1916, were a total anti-climax compared to Henry's previous electoral experiences. There was an indifferent response to the poll. At Kilrea, only forty Nationalists had voted by six o'clock, and at Garvagh only five or six polled.[37] Some Nationalists openly declared for Henry.[38] While Henry had motor vehicles at his disposal, tally rooms and an impersonating agent, it was reported that Turnball had none of these.[39] The count lasted for one hundred minutes, with the following result:

> Henry (Unionist) 3,808
> Turnball (Indep.) 214

There were 17 spoiled votes, and Denis Henry was now Unionist MP for South Derry by a margin of 3,594 votes.[40]

Like his previous contests, South Derry sheds more light on contemporary attitudes to Denis Henry. The size of Henry's vote suggests a solid endorsement from Unionists, and an acknowledgement that, even though Henry was now in his fifty-second year, had no parliamentary experience and was twice an unsuccessful Unionist candidate, his ability was such that he could still contribute to the Unionist cause. The Nationalist feeling towards Henry contrasted with the clear hostility revealed earlier in Henry's life. Some Nationalists voted for Henry, though this can be partly explained by a possibly more friendly atmosphere engendered by the truce. Yet there is some concrete evidence that Nationalist aggression towards Henry had waned. The *Londonderry Sentinel* reported that the Catholic clergy had not referred to the South Derry election in their churches, and it was said that one priest had told his congregation that one of the candidates was a Catholic and they might vote for him if they wished.[41] Among the many telegrams of congratulations sent to Henry after his election, was one from Father P. Convery, PP, St. Paul's, Belfast.[42] On 17 May 1916, the Rev. P. McGeown, CC Kilrea, wrote to a newspaper saying that Catholics should be grateful to Unionists for supporting

Henry, and went on:

> At present it matters not whether a man is a Nationalist, a Unionist, or a Liberal, but to us it does matter very much that he should be a Catholic. And Mr. Denis Henry, KC, is a Catholic. We feel that when our interests, or the interests of our religion are at stake, we shall have a supporter in our future MP.[43]

It is hard to envisage such a response from Catholic clergy towards Henry in 1906 or 1907, so why the change in attitude in 1916? Perhaps Catholics were by now accustomed to Henry's stance, and therefore less startled by his appearance on Unionist platforms. Or did the absence of a close-run election mean a more amiable attitude towards Henry, whose South Derry background made him more acceptable? Whatever the answer, nothing could alter the fact that Henry found it easier to stand for the Unionists in 1916 than in 1906. It was fitting too, that Henry's first election victory should be on his 'home ground'. He was very moved by the thought that South Derry was the area in which he had begun his professional life and in which he had won his first case.[44] On 29 May 1916, Henry took his seat in Westminster, introduced by Edward Carson and John Lonsdale, respectively Chairman and Secretary of the Ulster Unionist Party. The *Northern Whig* reported how Mrs Henry witnessed her husband's introduction from the ladies' gallery, and commented; 'Many observers were struck by the dignified and agreeable personality of the new member, and it was the subject later on of interested remarks in the lobby.'[45]

Shortly after entering Westminster, Henry's legal ability received a hint of recognition from the coalition government when, between 23 and 31 August 1916, he formed part of a three-man Royal Commission inquiry into the deaths of Francis Sheehy Skeffington and two other men during the Easter Rising. The Commission, led by Sir John Simon, former Attorney-General and Home Secretary under Asquith, also featured Lord Justice Maloney, the Lord Chief Justice of Ireland, with Henry playing a subordinate role. The Commission investigated the circumstances under which Sheehy Skeffington, Thomas Dickson and Patrick MacIntyre died on 25 April 1916 at Portobello Barracks in Dublin. Henry would have been well acquainted with the legal representatives of the parties involved: J.H. Campbell, Attorney-General for Ireland, represented the government; for Skeffington and Dickson, Tim Healy, KC; John Blake Powell, for the military authorities, and T.W. Brown, who represented two officers who testified before the Commissioners. Much of the Commissioners' findings dealt with the killing of the well-known Sheehy Skeffington, and after their six days of proceedings which saw testimony from thirty-eight witnesses,[46] the Commissioners exonerated the three men, focusing their condemnation on the behaviour of a Captain Bowen-Colthurst, a member of the Royal Irish Rifles, who had been wounded at the front and invalided home at the time of the Rising.[47]

The inquiry team conceded that Sheehy Skeffington not only had no connection with the 1916 Rebellion, but that he had no association with Dickson or MacIntyre.[48] It seemed that having arrested Skeffington, Bowen-Colthurst 'adopted the extraordinary course' of taking Skeffington with him as a 'hostage' while he went to search other premises nearby.[49] On the way, Skeffington witnessed Bowen-Colthurst shoot dead a youth named Coade, without any provocation, prompting Sir John Simon's team to note that 'it is a delusion to suppose that a proclamation of martial law confers upon an officer any right to take human life in circumstances where this would have been justifiable without such a proclamation.'[50] Having arrested Dickson and MacIntye at the premises, Bowen-Colthurst returned to the barracks with his three prisoners, and told another officer that he intended to shoot the three prisoners as he thought 'it was the best thing to do'.[51] Subsequently, the three men were taken into a yard and, on Bowen-Colthurst's orders, were shot dead by a party of seven soldiers who had coincidentally arrived on the scene. Bowen-Colthurst's later statement that the killings were justified as he feared that the men might escape[52] was unequivocally dismissed by the Commissioners, who wrote; 'There was no foundation whatever for any apprehension as to the escape of these prisoners, and no sane person who honestly entertained such a possibility as a rescue would have seen in it any ground for distinction between those three prisoners and the other detained persons.'[53] The Commissioners described how Bowen-Colthurst had been confined in Broadmoor Criminal Lunatic Asylum after the sentence of a Court Martial which had found him guilty of murder but insane at the time of committing the crime.[54] While there is no record of Henry's private views of this harrowing case, nothing could alter the fact that this experience would stand to him when, as Attorney-General for Ireland, he would have to explain the conduct of Crown forces under emergency legislation.

Henry's parliamentary career was fairly quiet in terms of participation in debate, yet between 1916–1919 he was twice promoted to Irish Law Officerships; Solicitor-General in 1918, and Attorney-General the following year. While his legal ability was beyond dispute, there can be no doubt that Henry's political advancement owed a lot to the requirements of a wartime coalition government seeking to balance the political sensitivities of promotion with the judicial, military and administrative needs of dealing with a post-Rising Ireland. In 1918, the newly appointed Irish Chief Secretary, Edward Short, successfully pressed the claims of a Catholic, James McMahon, to become Under-Secretary, 'as a concession to the Catholic Hierarchy, with whom he held close relations (as Secretary of the Irish Post Office), and to conciliate the home rule party, with whose political aspiration he was in sympathy.'[55] H.A.L. Fisher also saw the advantages of retaining McMahon, as 'He was a nationalist and a Catholic, and his loyalty to the Crown was unquestioned, and his popularity made him something of an asset to the Irish government.'[56]

When James Campbell became Lord Chief Justice in 1916, his successor as Attorney-General was James O'Connor, a Catholic Nationalist from Wexford, who had been called to the

Bar in 1900, and had been Solicitor-General since 1914. In the debate over O'Connor's successor, H. E. Duke pressed the claims of James Chambers, a Belfast Protestant, while Walter Long supported William Moore. When asked by Lloyd George, Carson expressed the view that Chambers had many years' experience in the Commons and said that it would be better if both law officers were not Catholic. His views must have had some impact, for Chambers was appointed Solicitor-General.[57] With the electoral decline of the Irish Party after 1916, Lloyd George became less enthusiastic about the historic Liberal-Irish Party alliance, and continued to take advice on Ireland from the Unionist and Conservative side of the coalition. Consequently, the latter were successful in their efforts to regain parts of the Irish administration as key positions became available.[58] This was soon reflected in the selection of a new Solicitor-General after Chambers died suddenly in June 1917. Henry, described as the 'moderate Catholic Unionist from Ulster,' was passed over, as were other Nationalist Serjeants, in favour of A.W. Samuels, 'who as a Protestant and adept at using his knowledge of statistics to oppose Home Rule, was given the position in the law office.'[59] Born in 1852, in Westmeath, Samuels had been educated at the Royal School Dungannon, and became MP for Trinity College Dublin.[60] He duly became Attorney-General in April 1918 when O'Connor was appointed as Lord Justice of Appeal, but Samuels apparently experienced the dilemma of having to pilot the proposed Home Rule Bill through parliament in his capacity as an Irish Law Officer, while at the same time being an avowed opponent of Home Rule. Henry's chances of becoming Solicitor-General were diminished by his public refusal to take the post on the grounds that 'acceptance of one of the Law Officerships would be an implication, at least, of his acquiescence in the Home Rule policy of the Government.' John Blake Powell, a Catholic Southern Unionist from Trinity College Dublin, took up the post vacated by Samuels.[61] In a letter to his son on 13 June 1917, W.S. Armour, the Presbyterian Home Ruler from Ballymoney, commented on the promotion of Irish

Law Officers. Chambers died apparently after contracting pneumonia and mumps; 'The two diseases were too much for a frame worn by hard work'. Armour had hoped that William Moore would have been preferred to Chambers, but remarked that 'The government could not dare to give him the place when two really competent lawyers like Chambers and Denis Henry were in the field.' Displaying some perception into government calculation of legal appointments, Armour predicted that 'Henry, being a Catholic though a Unionist, may have to stand aside again as I am sure at the present time the government would not wish to have both law officers R.C.s. I fear the chief secretary could not appoint Moore for the two reasons – that he is not well up in the law, his reputation at the bar being low, and further because he has been so violent as a politician, irritating the Nationalists whenever he got on his legs. Chambers was wiser in his generation at least in a matter of this kind. We must wait and see …'[62]

Whatever disappointment Henry may have had at missing out on promotion was short-lived. Justice William Kenny, a Catholic Southern Unionist, recommended to Lord Edward Talbot that Henry should be offered the vacant judgeship as O'Connor's successor. His letter reviewed Henry's political service and his reputation as a lawyer, which he believed had not been recognised because of his politics, and went on: 'It may be said that this would be the third appointment of a Catholic to a judicial position…within a fortnight – but even so, it would, I can assure you, be a pleasing contrast to the two others.' In fact, Powell succeeded O'Connor, with Henry in turn replacing him as Solicitor-General. It appeared that, while Samuels had recommended the Unionist Serjeant, Charles Matheson, Henry was appointed over the heads of all the Serjeants.[63] Henry's appointment was well received locally. The *Irish Law Times and Solicitors' Journal* commented that 'no more fitting appointment could have been made. Mr. Henry has long been regarded as one of the greatest lawyers and advocates of the Irish Bar.' A meeting of the North-West Bar in the Four Courts,

Dublin, on 28 November, 'conveyed our heartiest congratulations to our Father', on his 'well deserved promotion.'[64] In May 1919 the *Northern Whig* speculated that Samuels was 'said to be thinking the offer over' of a judgeship on the High Court, but the newspaper's correspondent believed that, with Samuels' keen interest in the forthcoming Housing Bill and Health Bill in parliament, 'it would be a matter of great regret to him to leave these measures in their present stage'[65] A few days later, it was confirmed that Samuels would be vacating the post of Attorney-General, while the *Northern Whig* of 18 June reported that Denis Henry 'will be the next Attorney-General, his promotion being regarded as a matter of course.' It seemed that Henry's likely successor would either be D.M. Wilson, T.W. Brown or even W.E. Wylie, who was 'also receiving influential support.'[66]

It was in the capacity of the newly appointed Solicitor-General for Ireland that Denis Henry defended his South Derry seat in the general election of December 1918. With recent revision sessions showing the Unionists with a four-figure majority, coupled with the electoral history of the constituency as well as Henry's own standing, Unionists were well placed to face any opposition. The South Derry contest of 1918 is particularly noteworthy, for Henry's success represents the last occasion in which a Catholic Unionist won a seat for the Unionist Party in Ulster.

The participation of a Sinn Fein and an Irish Party nominee in South Derry ensured that the anti-Unionist vote would be split, and that Henry would be almost certain of retaining the seat. Far from being a mundane affair, South Derry was fought hard, with virtually two parallel contests taking place. On the one hand, Unionists worked to ensure that the seat would remain in their hands, while on the other, the Sinn Feiners attempted to make inroads into the Irish Party vote, and replace the old Redmondite party as the representatives of anti-Unionist opinion in South Derry. So determined were Sinn Fein to achieve this aim, that they contested all bar one of the thirty-eight constituencies in the nine counties of Ulster in 1918.

The Henry campaign was helped by obvious shortcomings in Nationalist preparations. On 29 October 1918, the South Derry Executive of the United Irish League and Ancient Order of Hibernians met at Maghera to discuss the election, only to pass a resolution which disapproved of any candidate who did not have the endorsement of the Irish Party, and promise to hold a further meeting to take steps to 'safeguard the Nationalist interest.'[67] Further Nationalist hesitation was indicated by the appointment of election committees for each townland on 31 October,[68] the discussion of an election fund as late as 16 November,[69] and the postponement of candidate selection until 22 November 1918. Polling day was close – Thursday, 14 December.[70]

In September 1918, Sinn Fein had selected Louis J. Walsh, a solicitor from Ballycastle, as their candidate for South Derry. The absence of an Irish Party candidate convinced Walsh that the contest would be a straight fight between the Republican and Unionist cause. In his opening speech at Granaghan on 18 November, Walsh congratulated the local AOH and UIL for their 'patriotic act' in abstaining from the election and thereby avoiding a division in the anti-Unionist vote. He regarded the contest as clear-cut; 'England v. Ireland'; 'Self-determination or subjection.'[71] However, any expectations Walsh had of Nationalist co-operation were shattered when, on 22 November, a Nationalist meeting at Magherafelt chose M.J. Henry, JP, as their nominee for South Derry. Even with this decision, local Nationalists seemed confused, for the delegates agreed that in the event of Henry declining to stand, John Dillon, as party leader, could choose a replacement.[72] In fact, Henry did withdraw, and Professor Arthur William Conway, a mathematics teacher from Belfast, was selected in his place on 1 December.[73] With a split Nationalist vote (in an electorate of approximately 21,000 voters, 11,000 were regarded as Unionists), South Derry in 1918 became, in reality, a struggle for ascendancy between Sinn Fein and the Irish Party.

The South Derry Unionist Association unanimously selected

Denis Henry on 20 November 1918 in Kilrea Orange Hall, and the occasion saw Unionists express their feelings about Sinn Fein's 'intrusion' into South Derry, while Henry himself took the opportunity to clarify his position regarding his recent promotion as Solicitor-General. Dr H.S. Morrison, who chaired the packed meeting, described Henry as the most 'willing and efficient' representative the constituency ever had, and dealt with the Sinn Fein challenge in conciliatory and almost patronising terms. Walsh, he said, was from 'good stock', and was 'clever, honest and genial', and Unionists would place no difficulty in his way 'as he wandered up and down the constituency.' Henry, however, took Walsh more seriously, and said that his Sinn Fein opponent represented 'everything that was abominable to their loyalty and allegiance.' After acknowledging his support for temperance, and commenting on the importance of agricultural prosperity in South Derry, Henry cautioned his supporters against complacency, and urged everyone to poll.[74]

Much of Henry's speech was devoted against the background of his recent elevation to the position of Solicitor-General, news of which came after a month of intense newspaper speculation. On 6 November, the London correspondent of the *Northern Whig* disclosed that Henry had 'first claim' to Powell's vacant post.[75] The *Londonderry Sentinel* welcomed Henry's promotion,[76] while the *Times* remarked that no member of the Irish bar deserved advancement more than Henry.[77] The audience in Kilrea Orange Hall heard Henry recount how he had had an earlier opportunity for promotion, 'but it was cloaked and surrounded by conditions which would have made it degrading for me to accept, and he felt if there was any man who should stand first to his principles, it was he.' Henry said that if he had accepted this early promotion he would have acted 'in a contemptible manner if he had betrayed their trust,' and any honour worthy of consideration would have to come 'clean', with the support of 'his leader' and the constituency.[78] Clearly, this was Henry's implied reference to his refusal to endorse a

Home Rule Bill, which was being contemplated as a price for Irish conscription, which the role of an Irish Law Officer would have involved. Certainly, Henry seemed anxious that his promotion should not have an adverse effect on his election prospects, by reassuring his constituents that his elevation to Solicitor-General meant no loss of principle on his part. As events will show, Henry's fears were unfounded, for neither of his opponents referred to his new honour, while local Unionists became more endeared to the South Derry man who had achieved so much in the legal world.

The South Derry election of 1918 featured a large number of meetings as both Sinn Fein and the Irish Party strove to rise above the level of mere participants and acquire as many votes as possible. While the near-absence of reports on Conway's and Walsh's speeches might suggest inactivity, the regularity with which meetings were held by the anti-Unionists admits otherwise. By 5 December, the day after Henry's campaign started, Walsh had addressed three Sinn Fein gatherings at Maghera, Bellaghy and Magherafelt.[79] Conway conducted nine rallies in a twelve day period, and when one recalls that he only entered the contest three days before nominations were due, this was a considerable effort.[80] Speaking at Bellaghy on 3 December, Conway warned of the disastrous effects on the farming community if South Derry was included in a partition scheme to form an 'English shire',[81] while eight days later at Kilrea, he spoke in favour of federal Home Rule, with Ireland having the same status as Australia. There was some Sinn Fein heckling at this meeting, and a slight disturbance at Moneygeigh, but overall the Sinn Feiners and Nationalists conducted themselves properly.[82] With both parties matching each other (in commitment at least), the anti-Unionist campaign carried with it two detrimental side-effects. Firstly, with both sides equally determined to capture a position of self-respect in the constituency, a sharp division in the anti-Unionist poll seemed guaranteed victory for either side appeared unlikely while Henry's success was virtually assured. Secondly, the efforts of

Sinn Fein and the Nationalists gave greater impetus to the Unionists, who in turn visited many parts of the constituency to ensure the return to parliament of Ireland's new Solicitor-General.

The South Derry election of 1918 was the fourth occasion in which Henry represented the Unionists, and this time he enjoyed the benefits of being the incumbent, the popular and respected local man, as well as possessing a deep knowledge of the constituency's wants and needs. Henry's election address opened with the familiar references to the welfare of servicemen and their dependants, as well as the customary endorsement of the Union. Henry's programme revealed his awareness of feelings among his constituents, as he supported the representation of farmers on all boards dealing with the prices of agricultural produce, advocated a drainage works to end severe flooding in the area, and called for fair wages and better housing for labourers.[83]

Henry developed his election programme in various speeches made all over the constituency. On 5 December, in Magherafelt, Henry spoke about partition. He said that he felt deeply for his fellow Unionists in the south and west of Ireland, and stated that he would prefer to see the existing constitutional arrangement unchanged, so that Unionists and Nationalists could 'enjoy the blessings and benefits of the stable and firm government associated with the Union.' Unionists, he said, would never submit to a Home Rule parliament controlled by College Green.[84] On matters of local interest, Henry told a gathering at Moneymore on 4 December that small farmers and labourers should be assisted in the provision of proper houses, and in due time become owners of their homes.[85] Regarding ex-servicemen, Henry praised their efforts during the war, and asked that their womenfolk show their gratitude by turning out on polling day. Henry praised Coleraine's contribution to the war effort, saying that no town of Coleraine's size had sent so many men to the front.[86] In this respect Henry's familiarity is scarcely surprising, considering that he spoke on several recruiting platforms during the war, including one at Coleraine on 21 September 1918,[87] and another at Limavady two days later.[88]

Throughout the campaign, Henry received warm and wholehearted support from all forms of Unionists; from Carson, Presbyterian voters, local dignitaries, Orange leaders and women voters. At Henry's opening rally at Moneymore on 4 December, a resolution was passed expressing 'unabated confidence' in Henry, and this theme continued wherever Henry spoke.[89] The next day, at Magherafelt, a letter was read from captain F.H. Watt, Grandmaster of the Orangemen of the constituency, which expressed the wish that every loyalist and Orangeman should support Henry.[90] At Castledawson on 7 December, the Unionist nominee was hailed as 'a tried and trusted Unionist',[91] while the *Coleraine Chronicle* referred to Henry as 'that redoubtable champion of Unionism.'[92] Henry must have derived immense satisfaction from Carson's communication, which was read to the gathering in Garvagh on 6 December: 'You have ever been a most loyal and devoted colleague of mine, and I cannot sufficiently thank you for the help you have given me in fighting the cause of the Union for so many years.'[93] Eoin Walsh, nephew of the Sinn Fein candidate, recalled many years later how, at the age of thirteen, his uncle Louis and Eoin MacNeill, who stood for Sinn Fein in the 1918 election in Derry City, took him to a Henry election meeting in the Maghera Assembly Hall, 'half filled with prosperous farmers but few businessmen, it being a fair day'. Denis Henry's platform party consisted of, among others, his election agent, the solicitor James Brown, from Magherafelt, and Jamie Boyle, the Unionist registration agent. 'Even at the age of thirteen', recollected Eoin Walsh, 'I was not prepared to fathom the art and wiles of politics', yet 'I realised that I was listening to an accomplished and convincing orator, a sought-after member of the Inner Bar. He spoke with a refined, cultured Dublin accent. Judging by the applause from his supporters, he was well received.'[94]

The South Derry election gives an insight into the Unionist reaction to a Catholic on their platform, while Henry himself shed some light on his attitude to religion and politics, giving some indication as to how he was able to reconcile his religious beliefs with his political outlook. Dr H.S. Morrison said that Henry's presence in Garvagh Orange Hall was proof of 'their fidelity to the principles of civil and religious liberty for which their institution stood.' For Morrison, Henry's religion made no difference; 'they supported him because he had been unanimously selected by their delegates to carry the banner of Unionism.'[95] In a revealing speech at Castledawson Orange Hall on 7 December, Henry explained how his early life in Draperstown shaped his feelings about politics and religion. In reference to a *Westminster Gazette* report which described him as a 'truculent Orangeman', Henry commented, 'Well, if that meant that he stuck to his guns and was as good a Unionist as any Orangeman, then, well and good.'[96] Henry attributed his association with Unionists to their acknowledgement of his guiding principle, namely, 'my desire to live in peace and friendliness with all men no matter what their politics or creed.' Henry said that this principle had been imbued in him by his parents, who had instilled in him the necessity of respecting every man worthy of respect regardless of class or creed.[97]

Henry had instructed his supporters to work flat out and take no chances, and he led by example. Between nomination day and polling day (4 and 14 December), Henry spoke at eight locations. By way of persuasion, he reminded his workers that the Nationalist success of 1885 had come after a split between Liberals and Conservatives, and he cautioned against simply relying on a Nationalist division in this election to give them victory.[98] James Brown, Henry's agent, was equally resolved to eliminate complacency, and the *Northern Constitution* of 7 December contained an advertisement requesting 'friends' of Denis Henry to lend their cars for polling day and to communicate with Brown to organise this vital aspect of the election.[99] In connection with this, Henry made a personal plea for transport three days before polling day, and with the electorate increasing from 8,000 to around 21,000, said it would be like 'moving an army to the poll.'[100]

Polling day in South Derry was quiet and uneventful. All the newspapers commented on the high level of preparations made by the three parties, and there was universal agreement that the split Nationalist vote would see Henry returned. The *Northern Constitution* claimed that every available Unionist polled, and noted the ample supply of Unionist literature.[101] The *Strabane Chronicle* observed that Sinn Fein polled well, drew attention to some Irish Party defections to Walsh, and speculated as to who would be runner-up to Henry.[102] The *Derry Journal* reported 'some apathy' in some rural districts, though the report failed to specify among whom or where this apathy was evident.[103] There was a complete absence of any unpleasantness. When Conway drove to Maghera, in a car covered with green flags, a Protestant clergyman got a great ovation when he shook the Nationalist candidate's hand.[104] James Brown analysed the votes and produced the following table:

	UNIONIST	NATIONALIST and SINN FEIN
Agivey	538	104
Bellaghy	645	1071
Draperstown	400	1360
Garvagh	933	545
Kilrea	1119	759
Moneymore	1579	809
Magherafelt	2027	940
Maghera	1565	1550
	8806	7138

According to Brown's calculations, Henry would have a majority of 1668 votes.[105]

The result of the South Derry election was as follows:

Denis S. Henry KC (U) 8942
Professor A. W. Conway (N) 3891
Louis J. Walsh (SF) 3425

When the result was declared, Henry suppressed his delight

sufficiently to commiserate with his defeated opponents. Walsh and Conway, he said, were 'decent fellows'. The former was from an old and respected family whom Henry had known for years, while the newly elected member hoped that his acquaintanceship with Conway would continue. With a hint of remorse, Henry offered his apologies if any of his speeches had given offence. Conway confirmed the mutual good feelings which prevailed, and said that the election had been 'very honourable and straightforward.'[106]

The result bore testimony to Henry's relationship with his constituents, the influence of Sinn Fein upon Nationalist voters, and undoubtedly James Brown's thoroughness as an election agent. Henry's winning margin was 4,961 votes, and by any standards conclusive. Of greater significance was the anti-Unionist poll. Collectively, Henry's opponents mustered 7,406 votes, which indicates that many Nationalists either adhered to the Irish Party, or went over to Sinn Fein – but there is no evidence of Catholic voters favouring Henry.

Within a few months, Denis Henry, the last Catholic to win a Unionist seat in Ulster, would become Attorney-General for Ireland for the duration of the Anglo-Irish War. A new phase of his career was to commence.

The Parliamentary Career of Denis Henry
1916-1921

I

HIS ROLE AS ATTORNEY-GENERAL for Ireland between 1919–1921 placed Denis Henry very much at the forefront of parliamentary life and, as events will show, Henry was to emerge as one of the most hard-line members of the cabinet regarding possible moves for a truce with Sinn Fein, while at the same time he provided a resolute, if not always convincing, defence of government law and order policy in the Commons. The duties of an Irish Attorney-General were outlined as far back as 1855, and with some minor modifications remained in force until 1921. The Lord Lieutenant would consult with the Attorney-General concerning the appointment of Crown solicitors for each Circuit, while the Attorney-General would also appoint sessional prosecutors in each county. These latter conducted Quarter Sessions, while important cases were tried at Assizes under the care of the Crown Solicitor, with Counsel chosen by the Attorney-General.[1] The onset of the Anglo-Irish War brought new duties for Henry. The Attorney-General was to direct that cases under the Defence of the Realm Act (DORA) regulations likely to excite hostility could be submitted by the police to the government before any action was taken. In 1919, reflecting the increasing tempo of events, the Attorney had to deal with cattle driving, illegal drilling, proposed firearms legislation and prosecution for various offences, including unlawful association. By 1920, the Attorney had to advise on the law governing compensation to police killed in the discharge of their duty. The hectic pace of events in 1919–21 placed onerous demands on Henry's legal ability and stamina; the disturbed state of the country, the increase in serious crime and the introduction of martial law generated additional work, advisory and otherwise. Henry was also occupied with parliamentary duties, and was occasionally also obliged to attend meetings in cabinet. Among the matters he had to consider were how the law might be strengthened to cope with new difficulties, such as the problems of local authorities which refused to strike a rate, and the constant issue of securing convictions.[2]

Henry, of course, was not the only Irish Law Officer of note during this period, and he was assisted by two Solicitor-Generals; D.M. Wilson, followed by T.W. Brown. Born in Ballymena and son of a former moderator of the Presbyterian General Assembly, Wilson had been educated at the Royal Belfast Academical Institution and Trinity College Dublin. Called to the Bar in 1885, Wilson had practised in the North-West Circuit, winning the West Down seat in the 1918 general election.[3] Thomas Watters Brown was born in Newtownards in 1879, and had been educated at Campbell College Belfast and Queen's University. Called to the Bar in 1907, he became a KC in February 1918, successfully contesting the North Down constituency in the general election of that year.[4] Brown, in fact, became Attorney-General on 5 August 1921 when Henry was appointed Lord Chief Justice of Northern Ireland. The vacancy in the Solicitor-

Generalship resulting from Brown's promotion was never filled, and he thus had the distinction of being the last holder of the two Irish Law Offices of Solicitor- and Attorney-General.[5] Henry was also supported by the appointment of William Evelyn Wylie as Law Adviser, which arose from the number of legal problems that the Irish Law Officers had to deal with, and the fact that one of the two Law Officers was frequently out of the country. The position of Law Adviser had been abolished in 1883, but was revived in 1919, with Wylie's brief to act as a general assistant to the Attorney General.[6] Wylie, born in 1881, had been called to the Bar in 1905, and became a KC in 1914. Such were the pressures on all of the Irish Law Officers, it was found necessary in 1920 to employ M.D. Begley in a temporary capacity to assist the Law Adviser as well.[7] A barrister of some repute, Wylie had designs on the vacant Solicitor-Generalship following Henry's promotion in 1919. After his close friend Sir John Maxwell wrote to Lord French on his behalf, Wylie met the Chief Secretary, Ian Macpherson, who told him that the government's wish to have the Solicitor-General in the Commons made him ineligible. However, Wylie was quite taken with the prospect of the post of Law Adviser, and recalled: 'Macpherson was empowered to offer me the appointment at a salary of £2,000 a year with the right to practise as well ... I jumped at it.'[8] Within a year, not only would Wylie clash with Henry and other members of the cabinet over the direction of government policy, but he would also reveal his formidable powers and eventually exercise a considerable influence on the government response to the Anglo-Irish War.

As Attorney-General, Henry served two Chief Secretaries; Ian Macpherson and Sir Hamar Greenwood. A barrister, journalist and Liberal MP, Macpherson became Irish Chief Secretary in 1919, only to resign in April 1920 over government policy. His successor, Greenwood, had been a Liberal MP between 1906–1922 (he later joined the Conservatives), and had been Secretary for Overseas Trade, 1919–1920. Henry's work as Attorney-General under Greenwood dominates this chapter, but first it will be necessary to outline briefly some of the events in Ireland between 1919–1921, which made this period one of the most demanding passages in Denis Henry's public life.

The killing of two RIC members at Soloheadbeg in January 1919 signified the commencement of the Anglo-Irish War, and during the year the police were attacked for arms and ammunition, ostracised and constantly harassed by the guerrilla tactics of the Irish Volunteers.[9] The Volunteers were determined to fulfill the pledge that, 'Every Volunteer is entitled morally and legally, when in the execution of his military duties, to use all legitimate methods of warfare against the soldiers and policemen of the English usurper, and to slay them if it is necessary to do so in order to overcome their resistance.'[10] Between 1 May and 31 December 1919, eighteen more policemen were killed,[11] and there was even an unsuccessful attempt on the life of the Viceroy, Lord French.[12]

The pattern of 1919 was continued with greater urgency the following year, as Sinn Fein and the Volunteers strove to make British rule in Ireland impossible. Between 1 January and 18 December 1920, 176 policemen and 54 soldiers died.[13] Sinn Fein set up Land and Arbitration Courts in an attempt to supersede the British legal system and break down the power of British law. By June 1920, 'National Arbitration Courts' were working in 21 counties, and reports of Resident Magistrates showed that British law had broken down across 13 southern counties. The summer Assizes of July 1920 became a 'laughing-stock': at Sligo, 35 out of 40 civil bill appeals listed had been transferred to Republican courts, while at Cork, Galway and Waterford the Assizes fell through completely for lack of jurors. 'It is hardly an exaggeration to say that British authority, as distinct from mere power, was broken, and that any future British policy in Ireland could only be implemented by coercion.' Postal communications were disrupted, and senior Crown officials such as W. Redmond, Assistant-Commissioner of the Dublin Metropolitan Police, and Alan Bell, a magistrate attached to Dublin Castle, were shot dead. In the first six months of 1920, 16 occupied RIC barracks were destroyed and 29 damaged; another 424 abandoned ones were also destroyed, together with 47 courthouses.[14] Government response involved the extension of the Defence Realm Act to Ireland for a twelve month period, during which the Restoration of Order in Ireland Act, with wider coercive powers, became law. In March 1920, the Black and Tans came to Ireland, to be joined in August by the Auxiliary Division under Brigadier-General Crozier. It was these branches of the military who began 'unofficial reprisals', which subsequently became 'official and authorised' in January 1921. On 22 November 1920, nearly thirty people were shot dead, and a month later Tipperary, Cork, Limerick and Kerry were proclaimed under martial law.[15] Amidst all the violence the Government of Ireland Bill became law in December 1920, but there was still no respite for the government. In parliament, Nationalist and Liberal members constantly criticised the Irish administration; the Labour Party sent Arthur Henderson to Ireland and his report condemned the activities of the Black and Tans. The newspaper columns of the *Daily News, Manchester Guardian, Westminster Gazette* and the *Times* produced further indictments of the government's Irish policy.

Such, then, was the background to Henry's work in parliament between 1919–1921. His position as Attorney-General meant that the greater proportion of his work was devoted to all issues which fell under the ever-widening heading of law and order. Answering questions about allegations of misconduct by Crown forces, defending and explaining the application and nature of coercive legislation, and facing the anger of opponents to the government when Hamar Greenwood was often absent from the House, made Henry's position trying and difficult. The opening of the new parliamentary session on 10 February 1920 was marred by wild and inclement weather. For Denis Henry and his colleagues in the Irish executive, this was to be a portent of what was to come.

A hunger-strike by Sinn Fein prisoners early in 1920 created a perplexing problem for the government, particularly in the Irish administration. The hunger-strike, which began on 5 April, concerned prisoners in Mountjoy Jail, most of whom had been detained under the provisions of DORA, and without the conventional procedure of charges and a trial. The hunger-strikers were demanding political status while in prison, an immediate trial so that they could hear charges and answer them and, in the absence of these concessions, they sought immediate release.[16] There had been protests like this before, of course, but the announcement of a widespread labour stoppage in the south of Ireland in support of the Mountjoy prisoners, and its obvious implications for the administration of Ireland, brought this incident to the forefront more dramatically than before.[17] The government's reaction to this crisis was anticipated as providing an indication of the official attitude to similar events in the future. The episode also reveals some of the problems confronting Henry as Attorney-General.

When T.P. O'Connor requested details about the Mountjoy hunger-strike from Henry in the Commons on 12 April, the latter was unable to respond until later the same evening, when contact had been made with Dublin Castle for further information.[18] Henry eventually told the House that there were 89 prisoners on hunger-strike in Mountjoy, and that 'some were nearing the danger zone.'[19] When pressed as to how many of these 89 had actually been tried and convicted, Henry remained vague, saying only that 'a number' had been convicted in the ordinary way by a jury. This absence of a specific number led Jeremiah MacVeagh to speculate that only two or three hunger-strikers had been tried, and that the government had no right to hold the remainder.[20] The *Irish News* accused Henry of trying to mislead the House as to the correct status of the prisoners, and the newspaper predicted that the Lord Lieutenant, Lord French, would be prepared to let the prisoners die, and 'the Catholic-Carsonite Attorney-General for Ireland has adopted the Viceregal attitude.'[21]

The next day, a more heated debate in the Commons ensued, with the government's policy of arrests on 'suspicion' being strongly denounced by Nationalist, Liberal and Labour members, and being stoutly defended by Henry and the Leader of the House, Bonar Law. T.P. O'Connor argued that the absence of a speedy settlement for the Mountjoy prisoners would prolong suffering and create martyrs, and he recalled the death of Thomas Ashe. Interestingly, in what was almost a personal appeal to Henry, O'Connor remarked upon the strength of religious feeling in Ireland concerning the hunger-strike, and he hoped that the Attorney-General would share the view that this was a serious element in the crisis.[22] Mr J.R. Clynes and Lieutenant Commander Kenworthy criticised the government's policy of arrest without trial, claiming that if evidence existed to suspect someone, then that evidence should be presented to convict.[23] Henry simply referred to the violence in Ireland, including the burning of 300 police barracks, to justify the government's procedure. The men who committed these crimes, he said, could not be brought to justice in the normal way, because witnesses were intimidated, and besides, getting evidence was not particularly difficult: the problem in these circumstances was getting it proved in court. Henry commented on the death of Magistrate Alan Bell to substantiate his point. Bell had been shot dead on a Dublin tramcar, in broad daylight, in front of dozens of people, yet no witnesses had come forward.[24] When pressed by Mr Clynes to explain the basis for suspecting someone of a crime, the Attorney-General went on: 'When a man of good position and character supplies evidence and makes it a condition that he shall not be brought in, because his life would not be worth living, the Government were entitled to deal with the suspect person by way of internment.'[25] Bonar Law took an even firmer stand than Henry, asserting that the granting of freedom to the Mountjoy prisoners 'would be to make mock of established law and order, and to foster organised murder and outrage.'[26]

The Mountjoy hunger-strike was the subject of a motion for

adjournment in the House that night, and considering the rigidity of the administration's stance in this matter, the proceedings ended on a curiously optimistic note from Henry, who hoped that the day's debate would have 'cleared the air', and expressed his desire to see the hunger-strike end soon without too much suffering.[27] Something about the tone of these words raised the expectations of T.P. O'Connor,[28] and moved the *Irish News* political correspondent to write, 'as the House separated there was a general impression that a change (of policy) was imminent.'[29] However, both the *Belfast Newsletter* and *Belfast Telegraph* apparently failed to see any significance in Henry's closing remarks, and merely derived satisfaction from the firm approach to the hunger-strike. This point makes the extent of Unionist disappointment at subsequent events more easy to understand.

On 14 April 1920, the Mountjoy hunger-strike ended when the protesting prisoners were released. The general strike which had paralysed the south of Ireland for several days terminated, and the Irish administration felt the anger of Ulster Unionists. The *Belfast Newsletter* reviewed the assurances from Henry and Bonar Law that the government would not release the protesting prisoners, and the statement from Law on 13 April, that 'no greater harm could be done than that any impression should go to Ireland that there was a possibility of a change in the attitude of the government on this matter', was held up for ridicule.[30] The *Belfast Newsletter* predicted that acquiescence in the face of the hunger-strike would encourage more lawlessness, and said that the government's decision marked 'the end of any confidence whatever in its dealings with Ireland.'[31]

An examination of Denis Henry's role in dealing with the Mountjoy affair gives an indication of the circumstances in which he was to discharge his duties as Attorney-General. In the first instance, Henry was unable to give precise details of the Mountjoy situation, even though the protest was nearly a week in progress. His reply to T.P. O'Connor on 12 April merely consisted of reading from a telegram obtained from Dublin Castle, and the probing questions from critics in the House indicated that the Attorney-General was unaware of how many of the hunger-strikers had been remanded, convicted or interned. This was to be only one of several subsequent occasions in which Henry was to appear ill-informed over an Irish problem. It is probably true to say that the fact that Henry was left to deal with the hunger-strike at all was due to the absence of the Chief Secretary, Hamar Greenwood, and if Henry considered himself unfortunate in this instance, then the periodic non-attendance of his superior in the House was something that he was to grow accustomed to in the following months. The Mountjoy hunger-strike came at an awkward time for the government, coinciding with drastic changes on the administration in Ireland. At the beginning of April, Sir Nevil Macready became Commander-in-Chief of Crown forces in Ireland, and Hamar Greenwood Chief Secretary following Ian Macpherson's resignation. As things were, Greenwood had little time to adjust to his new position, since he also had to contest a by-election at Sunderland, and could do little, at this time, to assist his Attorney-General.[32]

Henry also found himself adopting an attitude which was quite unpopular with some sections of the British press, as well as giving public support to a policy which some of his cabinet colleagues believed to be badly conceived. On the very day on which the hunger-strikers were released, the *Times* was condemning as inflexible the attitude of Bonar Law, claiming that his view 'was based on too narrow a conception and consequently wrong.' The *Times* urged that 'broader and more merciful considerations should be permitted in this instance to prevail', in order to prevent the deaths of hunger-strikers which would in turn boost support for those involved in violence.[33] Perhaps the writer of this editorial had some authentic source, for on 14 April the same opinions were expressed at a cabinet meeting which discussed the condition of the Mountjoy prisoners. Bonar Law was concerned about the prisoners' health, and was disappointed that Lord French had made no effort to discriminate in the treatment of those who had been tried and those who had not. Henry, along with Macready, believed that the whole affair was being 'badly managed'.[34] These opinions made the decision to release the prisoners more understandable, and Henry's conciliatory words on 12 April may have been a conscious attempt to lessen the impact of the shock which Unionists and Conservatives might feel about the government's change of heart.

Despite his failure to handle questions efficiently over this issue, on a personal level at least, Denis Henry seemed to acquit himself well in parliament. Mr Clynes noted, with annoyance, the absence of senior government spokesmen from the Treasury Bench on 13 April, commenting: 'Clearly the Attorney-General for Ireland cannot answer for the policy which has been criticised, and I doubt if my Right Hon. Friend has had much...to do with the recent decisions of the government.'[35] This view appears to reflect a certain sympathy for Henry's position, and the Attorney-General's hint of a quick end to the hunger-strike prompted T.P. O'Connor to say that Henry did his duty 'with courtesy and with efficiency...I am sure if it were left to his good Irish heart and his knowledge of the Irish people, that we would not be confronted with such a problem.'[36]

One of the main effects of the disorder in Ireland between 1919-1921 was to render it impossible for the normal machinery of justice to function, and the government had the problem of devising emergency legislation and establishing special courts to curb lawlessness. With the IRA threatening anyone who assisted the British administration in Ireland, witnesses would not appear in court, jurors would not serve and judges and counsel worked under the threat of assassination.[37] The Alan Bell case is an example of witnesses remaining silent for fear of their lives, while Denis Henry told the Commons of how a jury, upon finding a verdict at an inquest, asked that their names should not appear in the press.[38] Even the process of claiming compensation was hampered, with justified claims being forfeited by individuals who were afraid to come into the public

17th February 1906

Sir

Allow me to thank you heartily for your support during the Late Election. I am greatly indebted to you for your vote and efforts on my behalf. May I ask another favour from you. Give every help you can towards the Revision. Every vote is needed, and if you know of a man who is a Unionist and can possibly get a vote, let the Inspector for your District know at once. Again thanking you cordially.

I remain
your obedient servant
Denis S Henry

28 Fitzwilliam Square
Dublin

Letter from Denis Henry, 17 February 1906, reflecting on his defeat in the North Tyrone election by 9 votes

PRONI: D 2298/16/1: Letters held by Wilson and Simms, solicitors, Strabane

Henry, as Lord Chief Justice, is seated in the first row, second from left, and is pictured with the other members of the Northern Ireland judiciary. c. 1921–1925

This photograph was deposited anonymously in the PRONI in 1964, which coincided with the centenary of Henry's death eye.[39] A more sinister development, from the government's view, was the emergence in May 1920 of Sinn Fein Land and Arbitration Courts, which functioned in the counties and were to settle 400 cases before the end of the year.[40] So, not only were legal and properly constitued courts being interfered with, but Sinn Fein was attempting to take over the task of legal administration itself. It was a state of affairs which prompted Henry to tell the Commons that Ireland was virtually in a state of war: 'It is not an attack on one party, it is not an attack on the Coalition Government, it is an attack on your nation. It is an attempt to drive your nation out of Ireland.'[41] Henry's subsequent endorsement of rigorous policies to crush Republican disaffection showed that these words were no mere rhetoric.

An early attempt by the government to reduce violence in Ireland with special legislation came in February 1920 when, shortly after the opening of the parliamentary session, the Commons heard the second reading of the War Emergency Laws (Continuance) Bill.[42] The principal clauses under discussion were the powers to extend the machinery of the Defence of the Realm Act (DORA) to Ireland for another twelve months, to suspend trial by jury for offences under DORA and to create military courts under two Resident Magistrates to deal with offences such as illegal possession of firearms.[43] The Bill provoked lively debate, and Henry was required to support these moves which would inevitably tamper with juries and court procedure. Throughout the debate, Henry's arguments in favour of emergency legislation indicated complete agreement with the government. The Attorney-General told the House that conditions in Ireland had 'gone from bad to worse so far as crime is concerned', and while admitting that DORA might not 'succeed absolutely' in putting down murder, it would give the government 'the means of protecting many an innocent man.'[44] Henry also attempted to assure members that the abolition of jury trials was not as drastic as they might believe. He spoke highly of the integrity of the Resident Magistrates who handled cases under DORA, referred to the safeguards concerning their decisions, and said that jury trials were not being suspended for 'ordinary' crimes. Besides, DORA was being extended for only twelve months, and could be revoked if conditions improved in the meantime.[45]

Henry's calm assurances about the War Emergency Bill left critics unimpressed. T.P. O'Connor delivered a powerful attack, stating that in his experience coercive legislation merely increased crime.[46] There was no justification, he said, for proclaiming fairs and arresting people for singing 'A Nation Once Again.'[47] The Nationalist member also commented that Resident Magistrates were the servants of Dublin Castle, and concluded that the impartiality of these Magistrates was open to doubt.[48] Henry's 'quiet' approach, playing down the significance of the Bill, angered Joseph Devlin who observed that the Attorney-General was acting as if he was presiding over a tea party.[49] The member for West Belfast said that coercion was unnecessary, since Ireland was not a race of assassins. Had not more policemen died during the Belfast riots of 1886?[50] The *Irish News*, rather dramatically, compared the extension of DORA to 'a sharpening of the surgeon's knife', which would force the bulk of the population 'into open insurrection against intolerable wrong.' The political writer of the newspaper dismissed Henry's performance in the House as 'weak and ineffectual.'[51]

Implicit in the government arguments in favour of DORA was the belief that violence could be curbed, but when it became clear during the summer of 1920 that the opposite was happening, the whole machinery of DORA was reviewed. In the nine week period from 3 July 1920 to 28 August, the weekly total of shootings, raids, woundings and killings increased steadily.[52] Moreover, the morale of Crown forces seemed to be wavering, for in August, Hamar Greenwood admitted that 556 police and 313 magistrates had resigned in the previous two months.[53] Denis Henry attended three cabinet meetings on 31 May, 23 and 26 July 1920, where the deterioration in security was discussed along with new means of tightening up on the administration of the law.

Greenwood and Winston Churchill believed that the existing legal procedure, i.e. DORA, was inadequate for overcoming lawlessness, and both made suggestions for alternative measures at the cabinet meeting of 31 May. The Chief Secretary complained that the juries in the United States would acquit any policeman who would shoot suspected murderers on sight, but this was not the case in Ireland.[54] Churchill, with some frustration, commented that there had been 200 murders – yet no one had been hanged. When he proposed that three or four judges should travel the country and do summary justice, Henry, who was to be economical with words throughout, informed the meeting that this idea had been put to judges 'some months ago', but they did not want to touch it. Churchill's retort, that three generals should do the job, remained unanswered by the Attorney-General, but was to be indicative of the cabinet's mood.[55]

The discussion switched to other alternatives for keeping order. Lloyd George, who favoured death by hanging for violent crime and outrages, pressed Henry as to whether convictions could be obtained from Catholics. Henry's response was a flat 'No',[56] and when queried by the Prime Minister as to whether there were any 'lapsed powers' in former acts which could be revived, Henry's quick survey of powers under the Balfour Act, Spencer Act and Forster Act held out little hope.[57] Churchill inquired as to the feasibility of 'striking a particular area' and making 'life intolerable' there, but Henry said that 10,000 raids had been made in a six month period, and went on, 'We did not get hold of the revolvers. They bury them in bogs and use other ways of concealment.'[58] It was an unsatisfactory meeting; some cabinet members merely gave vent to their feelings, and their discussion seemed to go in circles. Yet some pointers did emerge. There was a general agreement that the DORA Regulations were incomplete and while prisoners could be tried by courts martial for offences specified in those Regulations, there were many punishable offences which did not come within their scope.

Henry, by drawing attention to some of the realities of the situation, had indicated that if courts martial were set up to try civilians, Catholics would not co-operate in seeing men hang, and no Irish judge would serve. Therefore, if new courts martial with power of conferring the death penalty were established, then the military would have to take charge. Whatever reservation Lloyd George may have had about this, there seemed no other way out.[59]

In July 1920, therefore, the cabinet discussions of the previous week became encapsulated into the Restoration of Order in Ireland Bill, which was introduced into the Commons and became law on 12 August.[60] The Act proposed that courts martial be supervised by the military authorities with power of death penalty. Coroners' inquests were replaced by military courts of inquiry, individuals could be arrested by the military authorities and districts could be placed under curfew.[61] During the Committee stage of the Restoration of Order Bill on 6 August 1920, Henry told the House that the government wanted the Bill 'because we cannot go so far under the Defence of the Realm Act as we can go under this Bill.'[62] Greenwood claimed that the time had come to replace the existing courts martial which, because of 'terror and intimidation', had failed to do their duty.[63] The *Irish News* pointed out that making soldiers judges was a grave mistake, since reports from the south of Ireland demonstrated that the military were losing their discipline. Besides, the newspaper asked how officers, who were not legally trained, could possibly listen to and assess evidence which could lose a man's life.[64] Incensed by the Bill, and angry at the absence of Bonar Law and Lloyd George from the debate, Joseph Devlin repeatedly interrupted government spokesmen, and was asked to withdraw by the Speaker. Standing his ground – 'I will remain as long as I choose, and I will use every weapon for the purpose of letting the world know the dangerous transaction you are carrying on' – Devlin refused to move even when the Sergeant-at-Arms approached, and left the House only when a motion was passed requesting him to do so.[65]

William Wylie's role as Law Adviser highlighted government divisions over Irish policy, while cabinet minutes reveal that Henry's firm endorsement of coercion was quite consistent both in private as well as in public. While a section of the cabinet like French believed that the whole Sinn Fein/Volunteer movement had to be destroyed by means of martial law and a declaration of war, Wylie concluded that military measures would only worsen the chances of a final settlement in Ireland unless they were accompanied by some realistic constitutional measures. In this thesis Wylie was supported, to varying degrees, by several members of the Irish administration: Sir John Anderson (Joint Under Secretary to the Lord Lieutenant), Alfred Cope (Assistant Under Secretary for Ireland) and Mark Sturgis (Joint Assistant Secretary for Ireland). H.A.L. Fisher, while accepting the 'murder gang' theory, instinctively inclined to the sort of solution advocated by Wylie, Cope and Sturgis. Even Macready's views came close to Wylie's, as he told Lloyd George in May 1920 that Sinn Fein contained many men of substance and deep feelings, and could not be dismissed as a party of murderers. Wylie shaped the thinking of this 'Castle Group': 'Wylie was loyal both to Ireland and to the legal system, and was torn between a hatred of coercion and a desire to uphold the sanctity of the law'. In May 1920 he told Greenwood, 'British law was framed for a constitutional principle by a constitutional people. Its ultimate sanction is the people. In any democratic country that is so and the root reason why the present administration of Ireland is so difficult is that there is no body of people behind the administration.'[66]

At a heated cabinet conference on 23 July 1920, which Henry attended, Wylie 'opened with a brilliant speech', describing the breakdown of the legal system in Ireland, and calling for negotiations with Sinn Fein. He asked the cabinet not to refuse to talk to 'murderers', for the rebels, he said, 'were not committing outrages through blood-lust, but because they believed that they had been tricked by the British Government, and the only way to focus the eyes of Europe on their cause was by the adoption of these methods.' Wylie also claimed that the RIC would be 'little better than a mob', capable only of terrorism, so that the government would be unable to restore the law.[67] The meeting reached no positive conclusions, and its aftermath saw nearly all the combatants firmly entrenched in their original positions. Wylie clashed with Churchill over the direction of government policy, and afterwards Denis Henry told the Law Adviser how, after he had departed, Balfour had remarked that 'that young man has lost his nerve'. 'I wish', observed Wylie, 'that they had been doing my job in Ireland for a month or two.'[68] This exchange suggested some intimacy between Henry and Wylie, in spite of their different analyses over the Irish situation. Later, when Wylie contemplated resignation over the Restoration of Order in Ireland Act and the 1920 Government of Ireland Bill, Henry urged him not to do so; 'all he had fought for was nearer than he knew, and to go now was suicide.'[69] However, not all of the 'Castle Group' were on such good terms with the Irish Law Officers, evidenced by a remarkable entry by Sturgis in his diary, on 26 September 1920; 'Campbell, the Lord Chancellor, was a poltroon of the most contemptible type, a man who did nothing and apparently thought of nothing but the best way to show Sinn Fein that he was neutral and passive. He is a coward and a shirker, and, by God, a thief too, since he continues to draw his salary. The Attorney-General, Henry, sat in London afraid to set foot in Ireland, while the Solicitor-General Wilson is a fool. Wylie was the only member of the legal bigwigs who was worth his salt.'[70] The scathing comment about Henry's personal courage perhaps owed more to Sturgis' frustrations than anything else, for within twelve months Henry had accepted the position of the first Lord Chief Justice of Northern Ireland, which in the circumstances was scarcely a low profile role to take.

When the cabinet conference of 23 July discussed the question of negotiations with Sinn Fein, Denis Henry disagreed with the experts as to the number of 'righteous Sinn Feiners', and did not think that it was '90% of the total'. Henry's view was that the 'bad element' in Sinn Fein would seize on any new statement made by the government, and that any Sinn Feiners who dared to come to the negotiating table would be shot; 'On the other hand, if there were some way by which the 75 elected representatives of Sinn Fein could meet and give an undertaking, the position would be materially changed.'[71] On 27 April 1921, Henry agreed with the majority cabinet view that the elections in the south of Ireland, due to be held under the 1920 Government of Ireland Act, should not be postponed, even if a newly elected Sinn Fein Parliament failed to function properly; 'therefore you dissolve it, get Crown Colony government and postpone as long as you like.'[72] During another cabinet debate on the question of making a truce offer to Sinn Fein, Henry shared the view outlined by the Catholic Lord Lieutenant, Fitz Alan, who said, 'you can't make a truce without meeting Michael Collins. We can't have that. We can't take the initiative and must hope that they will'. The cabinet voted by nine to five on 12 May 1921 not to offer a truce, with Henry and Fitz Alan supporting, among others, the majority view of Lloyd George and Balfour.[73]

Several debates in May 1921, a few weeks before Henry left the Commons to become Lord Chief Justice, summarise effectively his determination to endorse emergency legislation during the Anglo-Irish War. The focus of discussion centred around the fate of Patrick Casey who, following his arrest immediately after an ambush on a military patrol in a martial law area (Mitchelstown, Co. Cork), was tried and executed in little over twenty-four hours, between 1 and 2 May. Casey was the first instance of trial by what was known as a 'Drumhead' Court, which arose out of instructions to the military to administer summary justice in martial law districts within a narrow time limit: 'It seems likely that one reason for this procedure was that the speed and circumstances of the process prevented the accused from obtaining legal representation and thus from challenging the proceedings in the civil courts'.[74] A person arrested, for example, in the possession of arms and explosives could find himself subject to an application made to the nearest officer not under the rank of Field Officer in command of a body of troops to convene a Drumhead Court. This was to be done 'where the evidence appears to be clear beyond possibility of doubt'. The Drumhead Court would be convened at the nearest convenient place, consist of three officers of whom the President was to be of Field rank, and no adjournments were to be allowed. Nothing was to be done to delay the commencement and conclusion of the trial, and if the sentence was death, then the confirming officer was to instruct its immediate execution. Since a suspect tried under a Drumhead was always executed, 'the proceedings could not be said to determine the guilt or innocence of the accused, since the decision to convene a Drumhead Court effectively prejudged the case, but rather to share responsibility for the fate of the captive.'[75]

Over a period of several days Henry was questioned by MPs concerned about the legality of the Drumhead Court, and the ethics involved, with the Casey affair being used to mount a wider attack on the conduct of Crown forces. Major MacKenzie Wood, Liberal, described as 'a sturdy Aberdonian',[76] asked Henry to reconcile the manner with which Casey met his fate with the assurances apparently given by General Macready a few days before to an American journalist, which gave the impression that murder convictions would go before the Judge-Advocate-General in London, who would have to be convinced of the legality of the verdict before any execution would be carried out. Henry replied that Macready's comment referred only to cases of courts martial under ROIA, and not to military courts in a martial law area.[77] When later pressed by Wood as to why the same procedure in courts martial was not followed in military courts, Henry repeated the legal distinction, sharply adding, 'It has been found after many years' experience that a summary sentence of the description mentioned has a great effect.' When Wood asked who was to decide if a person was caught 'red-handed' in order to be tried by a Drumhead, Henry tersely commented that such decisions were made by a body of English and Scottish officers, and in a more offensive mood asked, 'Does any Hon. Gentleman who has the experience of the effect of a rapid punishment doubt that a summary punishment is of great effect and perhaps the most merciful in the end?'[78] The *Irish News* queried Henry's statement that an application for the Judge-Advocate-General would have been 'carefully considered by the Court', pointing out that 'it is quite obvious that the Court was the final arbiter of destiny in the case, and that the members of the Court were in a position to deny the prisoner's supposed right to have his sentence reviewed in London, and that there was no appeal from their decisions.'[79]

Henry adopted the same robust stance when questioned by other MPs. When Mr MacCallum Scot inquired about Patrick Casey's crime, Henry, in a matter-of-fact way said, 'He was seen shooting at an officer twice. He was arrested on the spot, and sentenced to be shot. The sentence was confirmed by the military governor, and he was executed.' To the additional question, 'was he found guilty of murder?' Henry replied, 'My recollection is that he was found guilty of levying war, which is treason.' A requested assurance from Mr. Hogge that in future 'such indecent haste will not be shown' brought cries of 'withdraw' from government benches, and Henry must have been grateful for the Speaker's ruling that 'notice must be given of matters involving a change of policy as the question of the Hon. Member does.'[80] Captain W. Benn came closest to condemning the wider government policy of 'reprisals', claiming that the Casey affair had confirmed a growing 'well-founded belief that the Government is not desirous that certain criminals should be brought to justice or that the facts should be brought to light.' T.P. O'Connor had a notable exchange with Henry, and asked, 'could any military law in its literal interpretation be held technically to justify the execution of a man within 25 hours of his arrest? Even if it had been proved, the indecency and horror of the transaction would remain the same.' Predicting an overwhelming victory for Sinn Fein in the forthcoming elections in the south of Ireland, O'Connor went on, 'Could there be a more terrible or eloquent indictment of the policy of the Government than the fact that they have turned all in Ireland into Sinn Feiners, with the exception of the small Unionist stronghold of Trinity College?' O'Connor's observation was remarkably comparable to John Dillon's famous outburst in 1917, when he told the Commons that government policy was 'manufacturing Sinn Feiners.' Interestingly, and in keeping with the pattern of Henry's experiences, political opponents were still able to distinguish between the man and the policies he represented. O'Connor, in what seemed a personal observation on Henry, said that he did not know if the form of coercion being debated 'is the gospel of the right Hon. and learned Attorney-General - I rather think it is not, because he has been brought up in the great tradition of the supremacy of the civil power – but there are people in Ireland who are of the opinion that the only way to deal with Ireland is by cruelty … That is what lies behind the execution of Patrick Casey.' Rising to the challenge, Henry replied that he deplored coercion and martial law and, in reference to his own experience, said 'I have been brought up in the belief that free courts and a free jurisprudence represent the greatest asset a nation can have…as an Irishman it is a source of shame to me that our Civil Courts cannot function in the ordinary way, as they did for so many years when I lived in Dublin.' In Henry's view, government policy was dictated by the need to face the stark reality that 'it is the duty of the Government to proclaim a state of martial law and to repel force by force. Men who take up arms in Ireland are in a state of rebellion. They are rebels and they are traitors, and the Government of the country is entitled to deal with them on that basis.' In a clear riposte to those who raised the Casey episode, Henry asked, 'What time do constables and the soldiers who are shot get? Do they get 25 hours? Do they get the assistance of a clergyman of their religion, or do they get any form of trial? No.'[81] Henry's experiences as Attorney-General had certainly made their mark. A.M. Sullivan relates how, shortly after Henry became Attorney-General, he showed how much of a 'stickler for due process' he was by rejecting a plan to abolish public trials, and substitute in their place a submissory process which might result in the execution of ten or twenty known murderers a week until crime was stopped. 'Henry was appalled at my scheme', wrote Sullivan.[82]

One of the functions of Irish Attorney-General was that of giving verbal and written answers to questions in the House relating to all matters of law and order in Ireland. An analysis of the debates between 1919 and 1921 suggest that this was the least convincing and perhaps least satisfying aspect of Henry's term of office. The Mountjoy hunger-strike already demonstrated how, in the absence of the Chief Secretary, and lacking first hand information, Henry's knowledge of events was unlikely to stand up to close scrutiny, and there are numerous instances when the Attorney-General gave vague evasive answers, or simply ignored a question altogether.

In April 1920, an incident occurred at Milltown Malbray, in which a crowd celebrating the release of the Mountjoy prisoners clashed with some soldiers, resulting in the deaths of three civilians and the wounding of ten others. Henry's explanation owed itself entirely to a report from the appropriate military authority, and his comment that 'this regrettable incident entirely arose – so my information goes – from an unprovoked attack made by members of the crowd upon the patrol', illustrates Henry's difficulty.[83] There were to be many occasions when the credibility of his replies hinged almost entirely on the availability and reliability of military reports and sources in Ireland. When such information was either not forthcoming, or incomplete or inaccurate, then Henry's position would be awkward. Questions put to Henry on 2 December 1920 concerning murders and reprisals received from the Attorney-General the predictable reference to a police report, or a comment, such as 'I cannot answer that question off hand.'[84] On 28 November 1920, Lieutenant Commander Kenworthy put down a question on the destruction of creameries at

Abbeydorney, yet by 9 December Henry could still not provide an explanation, and merely responded that officers who made such enquiries were often shot.[85] Angry at this reply, Mr. Waterson accused the government of evasiveness, whereupon Henry retorted, 'The House can form its own opinion as to that, but there is no attempt on the part of the Irish government to evade responsibility.'[86] Interestingly, Henry did not deny the charge put to him, and even in the presence of the Chief Secretary was willing to acknowledge that the Irish administration had its faults.[87] As the violence escalated in the early part of 1921, Henry's days in parliament grew more hectic and uncomfortable. When Henry refused to discuss the alleged murder of men under army escort, his silence provoked a row, with several members, including Lieutenant Commander Kenworthy and Jeremiah MacVeagh, all demanding an explanation. Once again, Henry profited from the timely intervention of the Speaker who, with a remarkable statement , said that while the question 'may not have been answered to the satisfaction of the Hon. Member, it was answered to the satisfaction of the Minister who gave the reply.'[88]

In this context, the worst performance given by Henry came during the handling of questions relating to the serious outbreak of riots in Derry, in June 1920. The simmering anger at events in the south flared up into violence which saw several people shot dead, hundreds wounded and thousands of pounds worth of damage to property in a week of fighting which both Nationalist and Unionist newspapers called Derry's 'civil war.'[89] So grave was the disturbance that Colonel Ashley moved an adjournment motion during the Committee Stage of the Government of Ireland Bill to draw attention to the failure of the government to maintain law and order.[90] While Belfast journals were carrying details of turmoil, Denis Henry was informing the Commons that his thirty-five years in the North-West Circuit had taught him to regard uproar in Derry as an annual event.[91] Referring to the 'peculiarity' of the city, with its narrow steep streets, Henry said that order was difficult to keep, since 'there is no point at which a disturbance might not break out at any moment.'[92]

Many newspapers were furious at Henry's inability to explain why the police and military had failed to ensure peace and quiet, and the *Irish News* accused the Attorney-General of 'assuming' that the situation was well in hand and of deliberately trying to take advantage of what the paper saw as 'ignorance' in parliament about Derry.[93] The *Morning Post* revealed that, on three consecutive days, Magistrates had telegrammed Dublin Castle for help, which did not materialise until it was too late.[94] Henry's lack of awareness as to the gravity of the Derry situation, and his attempts at drawing on his experience of the city in order to make light of distressing events, merely accentuated the annoyance of Unionists and Nationalists at the lack of government action. However, the *Belfast Newsletter's* political correspondent did qualify disapproval of Henry with the vindicatory comment that responsibility for Derry formed 'no part of his brief.' The writer went on; 'Mr. Henry, of course, is not an Executive officer, and so cannot be saddled with responsibility or blame. One of these days the House will expect from Sir Hamar Greenwood a fuller explanation.'[95] The *Irish News,* in assessing the main differences between Henry and Greenwood, spoke of Henry's difficulties in parliament in this way:

> Mr. Henry can make professions of profound ignorance after the manner of a man who really regrets he has no information to impart, whereas his colleague's lack of knowledge is proclaimed with a truculence indicating great anger that anyone should be so impertinent as to ask a great man silly questions about murder and incendiarism.[96]

Henry was more at ease when questions and debate centred on legal matters or on legislative action regarding Irish affairs. Part of his brief was to expound the details of subjects dealing with compensation claims, fixity of tenure for Under-Sheriffs, increased salaries for Magistrates and the workings of the courts under the Government of Ireland Act. Henry was to acquit himself more satisfactorily in these areas in comparison with his performances already referred to in this chapter. A source of worry for the Irish administration during 1920 was the breaking down of the process by which claims for compensation were made for damage, injury or death caused by the violence in the south or west of Ireland. Hundreds of people who were entitled to claim compensation were terrorised from receiving their dues, and furthermore, many county councils were obstructing the payment of compensation to the military, police and their dependants. When Sir Edward Carson drew attention to this state of affairs, Denis Henry seized the opportunity to reveal that he had provided the Chief Secretary with a possible solution to the problem.[97] Henry said that a Bill was planned, which would extend the three day period in which claims could be lodged, to an unlimited period, and make claims more recoverable by placing claims on 'the same footing as Government debts.'[98]

The Bill, entitled the Criminal Injuries (Ireland) Bill, was further assessed by Henry during a debate on the policy of the Irish administration on 22 July 1920. The Attorney-General disclosed that, when the Bill became law, it would have the effect of compelling county councils to pay for outrages which may occur in their own districts. Failure to do so would result in a withdrawal of government grants to the county council concerned.[99] When E.J. Kelly, the Nationalist MP for East Donegal, protested that the withholding of grants would reduce the capacity of councils to provide adequate roads, schools and medical services,[100] Henry replied that the councils should foot the bill for atrocities committed against the Crown. He pointed out that if Sinn Fein terrorism was to be financed by the British taxpayers, 'there would not be a house or a haystack left in Ireland.'[101] While acknowledging that innocent ratepayers would suffer through the denial of government grants, Henry said that the guilty would be hit hard as well, and he anticipated that this fact would arouse the innocent 'to try and give every assistance they can to the Government of the country.'[102]

Henry was certainly more authoritative in defending the Criminal Injuries (Ireland) Bill, and when he introduced the Second Reading on 5 November 1920, and explained the workings of the Bill, the Attorney-General's familiarity with the measure and his confidence in handling critics indicated that he was more at ease when discharging his duty in matters of this sort. Henry told the House that, as things stood regarding compensation claims, a Judge would issue a decree for the money but 'a considerable number' of councils simply declined to pay.[103] Under this Bill, the Lord Lieutenant would be empowered to issue the decree, and if the debts were not paid, then grants ranging from £60,000 to £70,000 would be retained by the government. Showing complete familiarity with the subject at hand, Henry disclosed how the administration was still concerned about the welfare of ratepayers. The decrees for compensation would be spread over a number of years, say, five years for large payments, so as to ensure that the burden would not fall on ratepayers in one particular year. County councils would have conferred on them a new power – to borrow for the purpose of paying these sums.[104] The extension period was not, after all, to be unlimited, but instead of three days, claimants would have fourteen days to make out a case.[105] For Denis Henry, the underlying principle in the Bill was that legislation passed by parliament was the law of the land – and no council should treat it with contempt.[106]

Henry handled the interruptions of Joseph Devlin calmly and with some humour. Henry's promise to deal with Devlin's objections to the Bill 'because he deserves it' brought a large smile to the face of the Nationalist member.[107] When further pressed by Devlin, Henry declared, 'I have observed, even in my own profession and it is the same in this House, that when a man is being squeezed he generally cries out.'[108] Devlin's sense of humour was such that 'he beamed again.'[109]

There are further examples of Henry behaving with great assurance in the Commons. His speeches on amendments to the Government of Ireland Bill concerning the role of the courts or the appointment of judges to the Supreme Court of North and South were invariably long and detailed, packed with technical legal terms and delivered with insight.[110] When introducing the Committee Stage of the Magistrates (Ireland) Money Bill, Henry was well acquainted with the facts at hand. The Bill's aim was to increase the salaries of Magistrates and to make slight adjustments regarding their qualifications.[111] The Attorney-General described in detail the different classes of Magistrate, their existing salaries, and gave precise figures to show the extent of their proposed rise.[112] When a member pointed out that the salaries of other civil servants were extended without recourse to a Bill, Henry quickly replied that under an Act in 1874, salaries of Resident Magistrates were fixed by statute, and in these circumstances a Bill was necessary.[113] In like manner was Henry's treatment of the Committee Stage of the Sheriffs (Ireland) (Salaries and Allowances) Bill, which intended to give Under-Sheriffs fixity of tenure and an increase in salary.[114] Henry was unequivocal regarding the necessity for the Bill, and demonstrated a sound knowledge of the details involved. Altogether, this aspect of his parliamentary career seemed more rewarding, and the performance of the Attorney-General indicates a marked difference from those regarding his other work.

The Parliamentary Career of Denis Henry
1916–1921

II

L AW AND ORDER ISSUES did not take up Denis Henry's time
exclusively, and a survey of parliamentary debates reveals
that the Attorney-General for Ireland was a man of many
interests, though undoubtedly he had little choice regarding some
of the items on which he spoke. Henry dealt with various
legislative matters concerning the conditions of service of the
RIC, education, land purchase, the welfare of labourers and the
provision of housing for the working-class. These latter topics
provide a link between his election programmes in North Tyrone
in 1906 and 1907 and his parliamentary work, and indicate
some degree of consistency in Henry's attitude to social
problems.

Part of Henry's brief was to supervise and assist in any
modifications to the conditions of service of the Royal Irish

Constabulary. After 1918, legislation had been passed which regulated the wages and pensions of police in England and Scotland, and in 1919 the Constabulary and Police (Ireland) Bill attempted to place the RIC on the same footing as their counterparts. A clause in the Bill, preventing policemen from joining a trade union, was opposed by some MPs on the grounds that the absence of a trade union would be to the detriment of the police, as they could be liable to unfair dismissal.[1] The Nationalist member, Jeremiah MacVeagh, went even further, criticising the proposed pay increases as a bribe to the police in order to keep them 'smug and content' in the face of simmering violence in Ireland, and doubting whether an act of parliament was necessary for a pay increase.[2] Henry dealt with these charges very efficiently, explaining that trade union membership would adversely affect police discipline, and outlining the safeguards against unfair dismissal. A policeman whose conduct merited investigation would be tried by two district inspectors from another part of the country, while he would have counsel to represent him. Evidence would then be presented to the Inspector-General of the RIC, and the case would finally come before the Attorney-General for Ireland. Speaking in sincere tones, Henry commented on the obligations and pressures that this role would involve: 'it is a very onerous task, because I ... realise that a man is not to be deprived of his livelihood as a matter of course.'[3] Henry again showed his familiarity with the Bill when he told MacVeagh that police wages had risen on one occasion without an act of parliament, but this had come in the form of a bonus, and so was not a pay rise in the ordinary sense. Later, when Captain Benn opposed the Supplementary Estimate of £849,329 for the RIC on the grounds that the force was carrying out repressive acts under Dublin Castle's direction,[4] the Attorney-General stood wholeheartedly by the police. He praised their courage, especially in the face of recent violence, which he said marked ' a sad history' in Irish affairs. Henry went on; 'I am an Irish man born and bred, and I feel deeply for the dreadful condition of affairs that exists at the present time.'[5]

Henry's advocacy of changes to the rules governing police pensions provides another illustration of his interest in the RIC. During the Committee Stage of the Constabulary and Police (Ireland) Bill, on 31 October 1919, the Attorney-General drew attention to the problems which some members of the force were encountering after serving at the front during the Great War. A policeman, who having joined the army, could return to the force in the knowledge that his absent time would still stand for him regarding pay and pension. On the other hand, discharged and wounded men who did not rejoin the RIC lost that period for pay and pension. Henry proposed a clause containing the proviso that if illness prevented anyone from returning to the police, then the Lord Lieutenant could direct that that period be taken into account for the purposes of a future pension. In Henry's view, this was 'a very reasonable proposition'.[6] Henry's speeches on the Constabulary Bill reveal his characteristic ability to overcome legal jargon, communicate his ideas in plain language and in a conciliatory manner.

During the North Tyrone by-election of 1907, Henry's speeches dealing with the welfare of labourers and social questions were treated sceptically by Nationalists. However, Henry's genuine interest in social problems is manifest in his attitude to two measures in 1919. During the Committee Stage of the Working-Class (Ireland) Bill on 18 July 1919, Henry endorsed a suggestion by E. J. Kelly, representing East Donegal, that sums of £100 for the purchase of land by local authorities should be lodged in the County Court rather than at the High Court. The aim would be to reduce the cost of buying land for local authorities, with a consequential drop in the cost of plots for housing the working-class. Henry was involved in complex discussions over clauses of the Bill, when he contributed to the Bill's passing after moving the Third Reading.[7] On 1 August 1919, Henry moved the Second Reading of the Labourers' (Ireland) Bill, and made suggestions in a concise and confident way. Under various Labourers' Acts, over 50,000 labourers' cottages had been built and under the 1904 Labourers' Act, any individual whose wages were under 17/6d per week was eligible for a cottage. Henry explained that a rise in wages necessitated a re-definition of what a labourer should be; his ideas on this aspect of the Bill were well received in the House, and the Bill passed through unhindered.[8] Henry's work on housing matters did not end there, for in 1920 he was required to supply detailed oral and written answers on such items as the number of housing schemes submitted under the Labourers (Ireland) Act since 1 September 1919,[9] and the regulations relating to housing grants under the Housing (Additional Powers) Act of 1919.[10]

Henry had a mixed success when dealing with land and educational matters. His work in the former consisted of providing graphic answers to quite probing questions from Captain Redmond on the workings of the Land Purchase Acts from 1870 to 1909,[11] and during the Committee Stage of the Government of Ireland Bill on 3 June 1920, Henry was required to speak about the transfer of Land Annuities to the new Northern and Southern parliaments.[12] On education, Henry had a less happy time. Queries about teachers' pensions and frustration over delay in the Second Reading of the Education Bill merely received references from Henry to statements already made or about to be made by the Chief Secretary and the Prime Minister.[13] In the absence of necessary information, Henry wasted as little time as possible on questions about which he was ill-informed. When Captain Benn alleged that the Rev. Denis Murphy's version of Irish history had been forbidden by the administration because it gave a biased Irish view of events, Henry replied, 'I really do not know, because I have never read the book.'[14]

This latter remark was born of frustration and perhaps tiredness on Henry's part. It was in the middle of 1920, violence in Ireland was escalating, and Henry, now fifty-six, must have been feeling the burden of duties which were compounded by Greenwood's frequent non-attendance. Moreover, Henry was now away from home, living at Wimbledon, and his Detective Boden by his side was testimony to the very real dangerous times in which he worked.[15] The month of June 1920 gives an idea of Henry's workload, especially when it is broken down on a day by day basis:

Profile of Parliamentary activity, 1 to 30 June 1920:

1 June: no work in parliament.

2 June: spoke on the Committee Stage of the Government of Ireland Bill, on the legal position regarding divorce laws, and the powers of the Council of Ireland.

3 June: with Greenwood, answered oral questions ; participated in the Committee Stage of the Government of Ireland Bill, which was entering its fifth day.

4 June: no work in parliament.

7 June: dealt with oral questions on cattle-driving in Ireland.

8 June: took questions dealing with the government response to Sinn Fein intimidation in local elections in the South of Ireland.

9 June: voted in favour of the Second Reading of an Agriculture Bill; supplied written answer to question about the availability of grants to private builders of houses.

10 June: faced series of oral questions on Irish affairs; the awarding of a special medal for members of the RIC; government assistance for policemen seeking employment in civilian life; the workings of illegal courts; public libraries; teachers' pensions; the Education Bill; a malicious injury compensation case; the release of Irish prisoners from Wormwood Scrubs Prison. Written answers by Henry dealt with an attack on police barracks in Crossgar; details of the total amount of compensation claims for damaged property, from 1 January 1920 to 31 May 1920; Henry moved the second Reading of the Public Libraries Bill, which was committed to a Standing Committee; he moved the Second Reading of the Sheriffs (Ireland) Bill.

11 June: supplied written answers to questions relating to the advances made under the Land Purchase Acts of 1885 and 1908; spoke on RIC pensions; voted with the government on the Report Stage of the Ready Money Betting Bill; voted for the Third Reading of the Health Resorts and Watering Places Bill.

14 June: provided written answers on police pensions; the persecution of ex-servicemen in Ireland; gave an outline of advances made under the Land Purchases Acts between 1870-1909; the issue of a pension for the widow of Constable O'Brien, killed on 6 April 1919; voted for the Committee Stage of the Government of Ireland Bill; spoke on the powers of the proposed Council of Ireland over fisheries, and on the administration of the law under the governments of North and South.

15 June: voted for the Committee Stage of the Agriculture Expenses Bill.

16 June: answered oral questions on the possibility of prosecution after the 'Dail Eireann Loan' for Sinn Fein; alleged intimidation at local elections in Tyrone; gave written answers about a Sinn Fein court trying British soldiers; dealt with the regulations covering barristers or solicitors who recognised Sinn Fein courts.

17 June: gave oral answers on police pensions; recognising the gallantry of the RIC; the activities of Sinn Fein courts; intimidation at Tyrone elections; murder of an unarmed off-duty policeman, Constable King; a boycott of police in North Roscommon; land purchase.

21 June: oral answers to questions on attacks on the military; written answers on questions about the number of hunger-strikers released since mid-April; voted in Report Stage of the Increase of Rent and Mortgages Interest (Restriction) Bill.

22 June: oral answers on an attack on the Inspector-General of the RIC in Dublin, that morning; spoke during the Committee Stage of the Government of Ireland Bill; discussed riots in Derry during an adjournment motion to the above Bill.

23 June: oral answers on attacks on ex-service clubs; disorder in Derry; spoke during an adjournment debate on Derry riots.

24 June: oral answers on the number of entrants and resignations in the RIC; pensions for ex-members of the RIC; Medal awards for the DMP which are available to the RIC; Sinn Fein's seizure of 20 rifles in Lurgan; on Irish Health Council; Education Bill; teachers' pay and pensions; disorder in Derry; settlement of ex-servicemen on land;

written answers on police pensions and National School Teachers' pensions.

25 June: written answers on sale of prison goods and possible damage to outside trade; introduced the committee Stage of the Resident Magistrates (Ireland) (Money) Bill; moved Committee Stage of the Sheriffs (Ireland) (Salaries and Allowances) Bill; voted for the Committee Stage of the Blind Persons (Pensions and Expenses) Bill.

28 June: oral answers on education; Derry Riots; written answers on the amount of compensation for damage to Clare Castle Protestant Church; prison appointments; spoke during Committee Stage of Government of Ireland Bill; dealt with report Stage of Resident Magistrates (Ireland) (Money) Bill.

29 June: written answers on school teachers' pensions; total number of arms raids and number of arms found between 1 January–31 May 1920.

30 June: oral answers on numbers of RIC and DMP killed and injured between 1 January–15 June 1920.

Denis Henry's tenure as Attorney-General was varied and busy. He had little control over much of the business that came before him, for that was determined by events in Ireland, as well as the availability of his Chief Secretary to deal with subjects over which Henry had little background experience. A study of the parliamentary index for 1920 to June 1921 shows that the greater portion of Henry's work was done when Greenwood was absent from the House. Moreover, when Greenwood appeared in the House for more prolonged periods, the pendulum swung the other way, sometimes remaining fairly even. Early in January 1921, the correspondent of *The Globe* noted: 'I caught a glimpse of Mr. Denis Henry, the Attorney-General for Ireland, in Whitehall yesterday. Mr. Henry, a man of striking appearance, has been working enormously hard lately.'[16]

Henry was to have little respite, for during the spring of 1921, his name became associated with the highest legal position in the new Northern Ireland Judiciary – that of Lord Chief Justice.

Lord Chief Justice of Northern Ireland
1921–1925

THE GOVERNMENT OF IRELAND ACT, which passed into law in December 1920, outlined the role of the executive, legislature and judiciary in the new Northern State which would begin to function after the elections north and south in May 1921. A Supreme Court of Judicature of Northern Ireland was to be established, and the Northern Judiciary was to continue for the Six County state all matters formerly dealt with by the Supreme Court of Ireland which, till then, sat at the Four Courts.[1] According to the 1920 Act, the Northern Judiciary was to remain a reserved service, in that all matters relating to its functions were to remain under the control of the Imperial Parliament.[2] Judicial matters in Northern Ireland were to function through the Supreme Court of Judicature and a Court of Appeal. The Supreme Court had two divisions, a High Court of Justice and a

Court of Appeal. The latter was further divided up into a King's Bench Division and a Chancery Division.[3] In charge of all the work of the Northern Judiciary were five Judges, two Lord Justices of Appeal, two High Court Judges and a Lord Chief Justice.[4]

While Denis Henry continued to speak in the Commons right up until June 1921,[5] Craig and his colleagues were spending the spring period organising the personnel and departments necessary to facilitate the smooth running of the Northern state, as soon as the election of 24 May was completed. It was in these circumstances that the *Irish News,* on 14 May and ahead of its rivals, linked Henry with the position of Lord Chief Justice.[6] The speculation provides an interesting gauge to the Nationalist opinion of Henry's possible appointment. The *Irish News* acknowledged that while Henry was an excellent lawyer, he nevertheless might not 'want to lead a forlorn hope in Belfast.' The correspondent reasoned that Henry would be more inclined to remain at Westminster, if only Greenwood – 'who stays away assiduously' – and Lloyd George would come more often to answer questions. Henry, it was said, was uneasy posing 'as defender of the atrocities committed in parts of Ireland', and the *Irish News* wrote that Henry had imitated Greenwood's tactics of 'sticking to the written text of the replies prepared for him and sitting down, glum and silent, when pressed to give reasons and explanations.' It was rumoured that Henry would prefer Westminster, and delay a decision on the Chief Justiceship until the election results on 24 May 1921.[7]

The thoughts of the Nationalist press on Henry and the Northern Judiciary were to prove misinformed. Following the Unionists' capture of forty out of the fifty-two seats in the Northern Parliament, the announcement of Craig's cabinet on 31 May 1921 coincided with the more widespread views claiming that Henry was about to accept the position of Lord Chief Justice.[8] On 6 June, the day before the first meeting of the Northern Parliament at City Hall, Belfast, Denis Henry was made guest of a Unionist Club dinner in London, and newspaper reports were referring to him as the Lord Chief Justice designate.[9] One might assume that, amidst the excitement of Unionist electoral success, and the news of his own promotion, Henry might be able to relax and prepare himself for the hard task of leading Northern Ireland's Judiciary. In spite of his elevation to the Judgeship, Henry still had his parliamentary duties to attend to, and as late as 16 June was appearing in the Commons. With the possibility of T.W. Brown succeeding D. M. Wilson as Solicitor-General, and a drastic reshuffle of the Irish administration ensuing, it was essential that these changes should be achieved without too much fuss.[10] Perhaps the Irish administration had the events of April 1920 in mind, when changes in personnel had coincided with the Mountjoy hunger-strike, and now decided to keep Henry close at hand.

Before outlining the contemporary reaction to the confirmation of Henry as Chief Justice, reference can be made to another honour bestowed upon Henry at this time. On 15 July 1921, Henry returned to Queen's University, Belfast, where he had conferred upon him the honorary degree of LLD. Henry's achievements as a student at the old Queen's College were recalled, and Professor Baxter, who presented the Doctorate, described Henry as 'one of the finest and most brilliant' of the 'fine legal scholars and brilliant advocates' produced by the Queen's College.[11]

The Royal Warrant confirming Henry's installation as the first Lord Chief Justice of Northern Ireland was issued on 5 August 1921,[12] and the *Daily Mail* regarded the appointment as emphasising the complete absence of any religious disability to the highest appointments in Ireland. The newspaper pointed out that three of the most important posts in Ireland were now held by Catholics: Henry as Chief Justice, Fitz Alan as Lord Lieutenant of Ireland, and the Lord Chief Justice of Ireland, Justice Maloney.[13] Although the *Londonderry Sentinel* referred to the religion of Fitz Alan at the opening of the Northern Parliament,[14] the Unionist press generally failed to dwell on Henry's religion in relation to his position as much as one might think. It seems ironic that while much was made of Henry's religion when he appeared on election platforms in 1895, 1906 and 1907, this theme should be ignored or played down when he was being entrusted with the supervision of the judiciary of Northern Ireland. Perhaps contemporaries had by now grown accustomed to the Catholic Unionist, while Henry's presence in the public eye after 1916 made him a more familiar figure in Ulster politics. If there was a lingering suspicion that Henry's promotion to the highest legal position in Northern Ireland was at least partly influenced by his religion, then this can be dispelled by Unionist reluctance to publicise the fact for some propaganda point. Speaking in the Northern Parliament several years after Henry's death, while refuting charges of discrimination against Catholics, the Prime Minister, Sir James Craig, provided an insight into the political mind of Unionism regarding Denis Henry's tenure as Lord Chief Justice. Henry, said Craig, was 'a man whom everyone respected ... if there was another man like him, there would be nothing to prevent him reaching the same high position as was occupied by my good old friend.' Craig's additional comment suggests that religion had little bearing on the Henry appointment, for he continued, 'I have never yet known a country prosper where appointments to the judiciary were made on religious grounds. As long as I have anything to do with it, that aspect will never enter into my mind.'[15] While religion did play some part in the appointment of Irish Law Officers between 1919 and 1921, it seems reasonable to suggest that, in the absence of documentation, the choice of Henry as Chief Justice owed more to his legal ability and his stance as Attorney-General than anything else. The testimony of legal contemporaries who, like T. J. Campbell and W. E. Wylie, may not have shared Henry's political beliefs, admits that Henry was quite unrivalled in the Irish legal world. As the Father of the North-West Circuit, with an outstanding career in the Four Courts, Henry would have little difficulty in commanding the respect of his newly appointed colleagues in the Judiciary, and would be ideally placed to ensure the smooth running of the new Court system. Moreover, while at times Henry appeared to be on the back foot in his endorsement of government policy between 1919–1921, he nevertheless was quite tenacious in his defence of emergency legislation and the official thinking which underpinned it. In cabinet, Henry, albeit in a quiet unassuming way, was quite strident in opposing any form of compromise with those whom he regarded as little more than rebels bent on destroying the fabric of law and order in Ireland. Such a man would be ideal to head a new Judiciary, in an atmosphere no less frenetic, involving equally strident views when the enforcing of new emergency legislation was challenged. The London correspondent of the *Northern Whig* expressed no surprise at Henry's appointment, commenting that 'it has been confidently expected...there being general agreement in the view that both as a lawyer and a man Mr. Henry was the most suitable person for the post.' The writer commented on Henry's noteworthy career as a lawyer, and remarked that, 'although he entered politics later in life than is customary with most professional men whose ambition lies in that direction, his political career has been no less brilliant.'[16] The *Freeman's Journal* complimented Henry on his work in the Commons during the absence of Hamar Greenwood,[17] while the *Sunday Chronicle* deemed Henry's departure a loss to Westminster, where 'his judgements were not only weighty, but when put to the test they were found to rest on unassailable law.'[18] The *Sporting Times* threw a different light on Henry's appointment, and bemoaned the fact that clubland had temporarily lost 'a genial and portly character', whose Gladstonian collar and curly hair, reminiscent of Mr. Chesterton, would be sadly missed.[19]

News of Henry's appointment as Lord Chief Justice brought reassurance to Unionists that the machinery of the Northern State was being assembled with the kind of urgency necessary to offset Nationalist claims that the Northern Parliament would have a temporary existence. The 'conversations' between de Valera and Lloyd George, which had commenced just after the Truce of 11 July 1921, were still in progress, and with the editorial columns of Unionist newspapers reacting to any suspicion of a lack of determination on the part of the British government to stand by 'Ulster', it was easy to understand the *Northern Whig's* anxiety that no effort should be spared to establish all the departments of the Northern State as quickly as possible.[20] In this respect, the Royal Warrant on 5 August 1921 was welcome evidence for the *Belfast Telegraph* 'that Sir James Craig and his colleagues are going on with the task entrusted to them by the (1920) Act, without troubling themselves too much about the attempts which some newspapers are making to persuade the public that their tenure of office will be short.'[21] This last remark was an obvious reference to the sort of sentiments expressed by the *Irish News*, which on 6 August 1921 claimed that the Six Counties' Parliament was 'inherently unworkable', and went on;

> Appointments have been made carrying large salaries; and we now learn that the absurd Northern judiciary has been given a send off with the elevation to the non-existent bench of Mr. Denis Henry, KC, as Lord Chief Justice…Sir James Craig's Government cannot undertake any work with any degree of permanency attaching to it because they know that there can be no permanency in this Partition.[22]

Herein lies one plausible explanation for the lack of any Nationalist response to Henry's promotion; namely, the belief that the Lloyd George-de Valera talks would bring about the rapid termination of the state of Northern Ireland. An interesting perspective on the position of Henry as Lord Chief Justice came from the *Morning Post*, which believed that the organisation of the Northern Judiciary would strengthen the Ulster Unionists' position in any future negotiations with the British government:

> The Cabinet may have thought that so long as Ulster's judiciary was 'in the air' it may have something with which to bargain or threaten the Northern Parliament. But Sir James Craig's quiet persistence seems to have won the day.[23]

On the very day on which he was publicly announced as Lord

Chief Justice, Henry left for Wales, where he spent a short time with Mrs Henry.[24] Shortly afterwards, he returned to London, where he was given a farewell dinner by his Unionist colleagues in Westminster. The occasion was 'a demonstration of respect and affection upon the Terrace such as has rarely been given', and illustrated Henry's popularity in the Commons.[25] During the evening, Henry gave 'a characteristically happy' speech, recalling the previous twenty-five years of his career, speaking of his regret at leaving Westminster and his many friends there, and resolving to serve Ulster well. Henry was presented with a valuable antique snuff box, dated 1829, bearing these words:

> Presented to Denis S. Henry, First Lord Chief Justice of Northern Ireland, by his Ulster Colleagues in the Imperial parliament, 5th August 1921.[26]

It was anticipated at this time, that before Henry took his place on the Judiciary, 'a special mark of the King's favour' would be granted.[27]

On 15 August 1921, about one week after leaving Westminster for the last time, Denis Henry was sworn in as Lord Chief Justice before the Lord Chancellor, Sir John Ross. The brief ceremony, witnessed by a 'large and distinguished attendance' (including Sir James and Lady Craig, as well as Alexander Patterson Henry), was conducted at the Town Hall in Portrush, and the unlikely setting did not go unobserved by the *Belfast Telegraph* reporter, who noted that very few 'of the holiday crowds who strolled around the sun-bathed sands or enjoyed the breeze round Ramore Head knew of the epoch-making nature of the event which was taking place in their midst.'[28]

The fate of Henry's now vacated South Derry constituency provides an interesting and final footnote to his promotion as Chief Justice. The *Northern Whig* was angry at reports which suggested that Marcus D. Begley, assistant to the Law Adviser, W.E. Wylie, was being linked with South Derry. The newspaper was disdainful of Begley's credentials – 'If he is a Unionist, he has been very successful in hiding the fact from the public' –

and urged that the South Derry Unionist Association be discreet. The *Northern Whig*, suspicious of the 'jelly-fish' government of Lloyd George, whom it accused of working to betray Ulster, commented that 'the candidate selection should be independent of all Government influence ... a Government that parleys with murderers can have no claim on the Loyalists of Ulster.' The newspaper contrasted Begley with Henry, 'who never forgot he was an Ulsterman. At times when there was grave danger that the Government would betray Ulster he was ready to sacrifice his personal interests in order to promote those of his native province.'[29] However, the *Northern Whig's* concerns were to be unfounded, for on 29 August 1921, Colonel R.P.D. Chichester, who had competed with Henry for the nomination to the constituency in 1916, was returned unopposed as MP for South Derry. With Chichester's wife having been elected to the Northern Parliament earlier in May, there was the unusual circumstance of a husband and wife becoming members of two parliaments at the same time.[30]

By 1 October 1921, the 'Appointed Day' for the Supreme Courts of Justice for Northern Ireland to come into being, all the main positions in the Northern Judiciary had been filled. Denis Henry's colleagues in the Court of Appeal were William Moore and James Andrews. Moore, from Antrim, had been educated in Dublin University, and had been called to the Irish Bar in 1887, just two years after Henry. While Henry worked in the North-West, Moore travelled the North-East Circuit, taking time off from legal work to represent North Antrim in Westminster from 1899 to 1906, when he was defeated by an Independent Unionist, R.G. Glendinning.[31] Moore became private secretary to George Wyndham during the devolution crisis of 1904–1905, and later became one of Carson's principal aides in resisting the Third Home Rule Bill. Moore was appointed Senior Crown Prosecutor for Belfast in 1915, and two years later became a Judge of the King's Bench Division.[32] The *Belfast Telegraph* pointed out that only Moore of the existing Bench 'signified a desire to serve as a judge in Northern Ireland.' A

'Southern Barrister' conceded that there were others more eloquent and learned, 'but William Moore has, to a greater degree than many, the qualities of mind and character that make a really great and good judge.'[33] James Andrews, brother of J.M. Andrews, Minster of Labour in the Northern government, was thirteen years Henry's junior, and after his education in Belfast and Trinity College Dublin, was called to the Bar in 1910. Received into the Inner Bar in March 1918, Andrews had distinguished himself by standing counsel to numerous companies and corporations in Ulster, such as the Great Northern Railway Company, and by acting as arbitrator in many labour disputes under the Ministry of Labour.[34] Henry, of course, was well acquainted with his two High Court Judges in the Northern Judiciary, for D.M. Wilson had acted as his Solicitor-General, while T.W. Brown had succeeded Henry as Attorney-General.[35] An interesting retrospective on the appointments to the Northern Bench came many years afterwards when, in his autobiography, Lord Justice Edward Jones described Henry as a 'very distinguished man', who had served Northern Ireland as Lord Chief Justice 'by choice', having accepted the position 'as head of our judiciary in preference to a Lordship of Appeal which he was offered at just about the same time'. According to Jones, T.W. Brown was 'somewhat put out' when it became apparent that, although Attorney-General for Ireland, he was only going to be appointed to a puisne judgeship in the new Supreme Court; 'but William Lowry pointed out to him that he lacked the statutory fifteen years to qualify for the Court of Appeal'.[36]

Henry and his colleagues had much in common. With the exception of Wilson, all were Ulstermen. All lived through the rise and development of Unionist opposition to Home Rule, and all bar Andrews had stood for election in the Unionist interest. From a professional point of view, these men seemed well acquainted with the law in Ulster: Henry had dominated the North-West, Moore and Wilson had worked in the North-East, and their knowledge of the area would serve them well, now that they were in charge of an Ulster judiciary. Nor was

Denis Henry photographed at Stormont castle during Carson's visit in October 1923

PRONI: D/1507/F/11/1–16

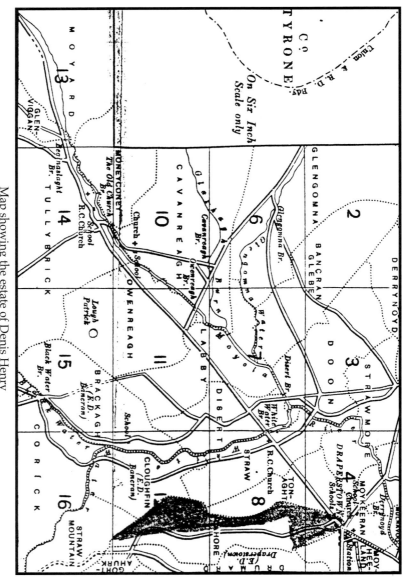

Map showing the estate of Denis Henry

PRONI: LR141. Will of James Henry and family members

their experience in legal and administrative matters narrow or confined. Henry had had a practice in the Four Courts, Moore had been a judge in the King's Bench Division in Dublin, Brown had served in the English Bar, Andrews concentrated in the North of Ireland, while Henry, Wilson and Brown had served as Irish Law Officers in Westminster. With Henry heading the Northern Judiciary, there was much optimism that this branch of the new state would function capably. Henry's appointment met with the wholehearted approval of his colleagues, and a 'Southern Barrister' assessed Henry in this way; 'The Northern Court is, indeed, fortunate in its first Lord Chief Justice. Mr. Henry is a man of most brilliant gifts, and it is no secret that the Bar expects great things of him on the Bench.'[37] By 1925, the full list of Benchers of King's Inns, in order of admission, was as follows;

> Sir Denis S. Henry: T 1898
> Robert F. Harrison, KC E 1904
> S. L. Brown, KC M 1905
> Lord Justice Moore. E 1910
> Sergeant Hanna M 1916
> Richard Best, KC, MP, Attorney-General T 1918
> John Leech, KC T 1919
> Lord Justice Andrews H 1920
> John M. Whitaker, KC E 1921
> Edward S. Murphy, KC T 1921
> Mr. Justice Wilson E 1910 and M 1921
> Mr. Justice Brown H 1922
> John McGonigal KC I 1923
> A. B. Babington, KC M 1924
> T. J. Campbell, KC M 1924.[38]

In addition to the appointment of senior judges, other important aspects of the Northern Judiciary were dealt with at this time. The Courts were to be organised into two chief departments, one of Register, the other of Chief Clerk, and as was the case hitherto, experience and a proven record of success appeared to be the criteria for these appointments. J.M. Davies, who was Registrar, was born in the same year as Denis Henry, and also came from County Derry. Educated in Dublin, Davies qualified as a solicitor in 1888 and practised mainly in the Four Courts, and in 1920 had acted as Registrar to William Moore in his capacity as the Sixth Justice of the King's Bench Division.[39] As Registrar, he was responsible for dealing with the issue and sealing of writs, filing all pleadings and other court documents for all the courts, and entering and registering all judgements and court orders. Even at this early stage in the development of the Northern Court, Davies had made his mark, and it was noted that 'his efforts in evolving order out of chaos within the last ten days have been most successful, and it may be confidently assumed Mr. Davies will prove a valuable public official.' T.B. Wallace, from Dromore, Co. Down, was Chief Clerk for the Northern Court. An official agent of the Unionist Party for many years, and 'regarded as one of the soundest lawyers and shrewdest advisers in the profession', Wallace was a successful solicitor, and his practice extended all over Co. Down. Finally, the Recordership of Belfast was entrusted to Herbert M. Thompson, KC. From Cushendall, Thompson had been educated at Coleraine and Trinity College Dublin, and after entering the Irish Bar in 1902 became leader of the Session Bar of the North-West Circuit.[40]

Before examining Denis Henry's work as Lord Chief Justice, a brief note can be made about the main events in Northern Ireland during this period. Henry's tenure of office, October 1921 to October 1925, coincided with one of the most violent and politically uncertain periods in the history of the Northern State, which increased the import of the difficulties which Henry encountered, and made a speedy and satisfactory solution to these problems a matter of great urgency.

Doubts about the existence of Northern Ireland were freely expressed by Nationalists in 1921, and were accentuated by the Treaty talks of October-December that year, and were only dispelled by the Boundary Commission's findings in 1925. The intervening period saw much unrest in the province, with attacks by the IRA provoking reprisals which resulted in 'the sudden death of innocent people in revenge for something in which they had no part and of which they knew little or nothing.'[41] In February 1922, sixteen policemen were shot at Clones,[42] and in May police barracks were attacked on the border.[43] Between 21 June 1920 and 18 June 1922, 428 people died and 1766 were wounded.[44] In 1922, damage to property was estimated at £3 million.[45] A point of particular relevance here is the fact that before the Belfast City Commissioners in 1922, there were 97 cases for murder, 59 of attempted murder and 37 of felonies endangering life.[46]

To overcome lawlessness, Craig's government deployed more security forces, introduced special legislation, and even entered into negotiations with Michael Collins. The Ulster Special Constabulary, formed in 1920 to assist the RIC,[47] was re-organised and placed under the control of the Minister of Home Affairs in 1922.[48] The RUC was formed on 1 June 1922,[49] and at this time there were a total of 50,000 full and part-time policemen in Northen Ireland.[50] The Special Powers Act, which received the Royal Assent on 7 April 1922, transferred 'many of the powers for preserving peace and maintaining order from the judiciary to the executive.'[51] The Minister of Home Affairs had the power to issue regulations for, among others, arrest without trial, and the banning of meetings and publications.[52] Later, provisions for internment were added, and internment was introduced in May 1922.[53] Curfews were imposed under the Act, and Belfast remained under curfew until Christmas 1924.[54] Craig met Collins three times early in 1922 to seek ways of ending the violence, with the final meeting resulting in agreements for the ending of IRA activities in the north in return for the enrolment of Catholics in the RUC, the establishment of a specially constituted court for trial without jury and the creation of a committee of Catholics and Protestants to investigate complaints over 'outrages'.[55] However violence continued, and representatives of Ulster Nationalists boycotted the new state in their own way. The Archbishop of Armagh, Cardinal Logue, had declined Craig's invitation to be present at the opening of the Northern Parliament,[56] while Nationalist members refused to attend Parliament until March 1925.[57] To make the depressing picture more complete, a post-war slump saw Northern Ireland with 78,000 unemployed, and 25,000 working short time.[58]

In some respects the period 1921–1925 resembled the short duration of Denis Henry's Attorney-Generalship: eventful, hazardous, hectic and placing onerous demands upon those in high positions of responsibility. A pleasing departure from this comparison was the fact that Henry was head of the Judiciary, and not a subordinate whose credibility often hinged on parliamentary answers based on hastily contrived information. As Chief Justice, Henry could direct and initiate, and his worthiness would now depend on the speed with which the first Northern Ireland judiciary functioned, and on the manner in which justice was imparted.

Most of the available information dealing with Henry's role as Chief Justice is located in a detailed memorandum entitled

Memorandum on the setting up of the Supreme Court of Judicature in Northern Ireland, and other matters incidental thereto.[59]

The document was written by Lord Justice Moore during the early days of the new Judiciary, and specifically concerns itself with the period 1 October 1921 to 31 July 1922.[60] Moore compiled this Memorandum in his capacity as Lord Justice of Appeal, so that the opinions expressed are those of an informed legal contemporary who worked alongside Henry and who would have been ideally placed to observe the complexities of the new Judiciary. Moreover, as if to lend more worth to the document, Moore noted that his report 'has been carefully read over, corrected, and approved by the Lord Chief Justice of Northern Ireland.'[61] Moreover, when one considers Moore's intentions in writing his Memorandum – 'so that the public in Northern Ireland should have before them in this statement a short account of the work done and the difficulties surmounted during the past ten months' – the end product could scarcely be more appropriate for the requirements of this chapter.[62]

One of the first problems facing Henry was to ensure that the Northern Ireland Supreme Court opened on 1 October 1921, the 'appointed day' laid down by the Orders in Council on which the Northern Courts would officially come into existence. Moore's Memorandum reveals that this apparently mundane provision was not fulfilled in as straightforward a manner as one might expect.

Denis Henry was appointed Lord Chief Justice more than a month before the courts were supposed to open.[63] Moore, who was already a Judge of King's Bench Division in Dublin, applied to be transferred to the Northern Judicature[64] – only one of the existing members of the Irish Bench who sought a judgeship in Northern Ireland.[65] Henry approved his transfer immediately after 1 September 1921,[66] thereby showing from the outset an interest in the confirming or conferring of appointments. Henry came to Belfast on 8 September 1921; the 'appointed day' was now three weeks hence. Henry had no other colleague except Moore, no officials and no courthouse.[67]

Henry was one of the principal figures involved in securing premises to house the Supreme Court of Northern Ireland by 1 October 1921. Under sec. (1) (b) of the 1920 Government of Ireland Act, the Imperial government was obliged to provide and equip a proper building for the Supreme Court.[68] Even if this responsibility was undertaken with the best possible intentions and energy, nothing could alter the fact that acquiring a site and erecting a suitable building would take time – something which was not on the side of the Northern Judiciary. A possible temporary solution appeared in the form of the County Courthouse, Crumlin Road, Belfast, which was owned by Antrim County Council and the Corporation of Belfast.[69] The courthouse was more suitable for its intended purpose – namely, Assize work of a fortnight's duration – rather than the more permanent departmental work of a High Court. Yet despite this obvious shortcoming, and the fact that the bulk of the Antrim County Council's business, as well as that of the Land Registry and

Belfast Local Bankruptcy Court, was conducted at the County Courthouse, this building seemed to offer the only way out of a dilemma which required speedy resolve.[70] Henry engaged in a series of meetings and correspondence to procure the County Courthouse for the Northern Judiciary. Firstly, he met representatives of the Antrim County Council, and received an encouraging promise of co-operation and an assurance that a sub-committee would be set up to deal with the situation.[71] Then Henry consulted the Lord Mayor of Belfast and the Town Clerk, and as a result of this meeting, the business of Belfast Corporation was moved to the old Recorder's Court, Belfast, a transfer which eased the demands on the County Courthouse building.[72]

Any optimism that Henry might have derived from this progress evaporated when the Antrim County Council offered the Supreme Court of Northern Ireland limited use of their courthouse building – namely, two courtrooms, two Judges' Chambers and one more room.[73] Moore regarded this offer with disdain, and noted that the Council's failure to appreciate the necessity for office accommodation for the Judiciary staff and members of the public made the situation 'a difficult one.'[74] At this stage, Craig's intervention proved productive. An agreement was entered into between the Commissioners of Works and the Antrim County Council that the latter should receive £2,000 for the use of part of the Courthouse building by the Judiciary until 11 January 1922, pending the arrangement of a more permanent undertaking.[75] Moore pointed out that Henry and Craig were reluctant to interfere with the workings of Antrim County Council, but Henry's 'imperative duty' to see that the Supreme Court was at least housed by 1 October 1921 overrode any other considerations.[76] The issue of courthouse accommodation was the subject of 'many interviews and much correspondence during 1922, and by October of that year it was decided that the Staff Court would retain possession of the County Courthouse offices until the new Courts were erected.[77]

All this activity meant that Denis Henry was able to keep his important engagements on 1 October 1921, and the Supreme Court of Northern Ireland opened at the County Courthouse, Crumlin Road, Belfast (though the actual opening ceremony took place on 25 October 1921). During a short speech, Henry acknowledged his gratitude towards the Antrim County Council and Belfast Corporation, and confessed, 'we have had many difficulties in connection with the institution of an entirely new series of Courts and offices.' Henry showed his awareness of the deficiencies in the Courthouse when he apologised to the Press for the loss of their room,[78] but Moore gave a more forthright survey of the facilities available to the Supreme Court when he wrote:

> ...it must be frankly stated that the Staff of the Courts at present are cramped and crowded and are carrying on their multifarious duties for the most part at considerable inconvenience, but they have loyally accepted the situation, and the thanks of the public is due also to them.[79]

Moore's observations were reinforced when a Committee on the Jury System in Northern Ireland, appointed in May 1923, heard evidence about the inadequate conditions in the Supreme Court, and went on, 'as a consequence much inconvenience and delay is caused in the administration of justice, especially as one of the two Courts in the building is required at frequent intervals for the transaction of the criminal business of the City Commisioners, Quarter Sessions and Recorder Courts.' The Committee reported that the Crumlin Road courthouse lacked a waiting room for jurors, and contained no separate accommodation for women jurors. The Committee's remedies included the installation of a telephone for waiting jurors, suitable kitchens and dining rooms.[80]

At first glance, the issue of courtroom accommodation may appear mundane, but in 1921, the very existence of Northern Ireland was open to question, and for Henry and Craig, the absence of a Supreme Court building could have symbolised the Nationalist assertion that the structures of the new state were impermanent. The level of violence made it essential to have a building in which serious legal business could be carried on. Faced with his first crisis as Lord Chief Justice, Henry could be said to have succeeded; he contributed to the acquisition of some premises to begin the work of the Supreme Court. Unfortunately for Henry, he would never live to see the new Law Courts building which exists today. Erected on the site of Chichester Market, the Law Courts opened in May 1933.[81] Work had begun during Henry's tenure of office, but not without mishap. A Cabinet document, dated 23 April 1925, contains a remark from the Minister of Labour, expressing concern about the slow progress of work on the new Law Courts.[82] This episode indicates the importance attached to the Judiciary by Sir James Craig. Although the judicature was quite separate from the executive and legislature, the premier was still prepared to intervene and support Henry all he could, and subsequent events will highlight this further.

Court accommodation secured, Henry could now focus on the problems of recruiting capable officers to work in the new Judiciary. This area presented Henry with three questions to solve; how to overcome legal technicalities which barred the way to conferring appointments, how to choose the best officers and how to ensure that successful applicants enjoyed fair and reasonable security regarding pension schemes.

According to Moore, Henry wished to introduce a scheme for creating court offices similar to the English system. There would be two main divisions, that of Registrar's Office and of Chief Clerk, with more minor offices concerning Taxing Master and Accountant General.[83] Though he had decided on the categories of his court offices, Henry was unable to set about appointing officers to fill these positions until the establishment of the office with its consequent salary and pension rights had been approved by the Imperial Treasury. Until then, the Lord Chief Justice of Northern Ireland could hardly nominate a messenger for the new Judiciary.[84]

Henry sought the co-operation of the Treasury in Dublin Castle, and had two interviews with Treasury officials in Dublin in September 1921, with one officer, Mr. Waterfield, coming to Belfast, whereupon after a 'prolonged interview' he approved Henry's scheme for court offices. Minor issues concerning trainbearers, clothing and uniform of messengers were only settled subsequently. Henry's discussions with the Treasury lasted from September to November 1921, and involved 'considerable correspondence and delay', at a time when speedy and productive decisions were needed most.[85] As with courtroom accommodation, Henry was again deeply involved, and must have found the travelling, meetings and correspondence quite taxing.

In obtaining experienced and reliable court officers, Henry was to have the assistance of Craig and Sir Edward Clark, an Englishman who became the first head of the Northern Ireland Civil Service.[86] Under the Government of Ireland Act, members of the legal and civil service branch of the Four Courts in Dublin were eligible to transfer to the Northern Courts, but many subsequent applications were accompanied by a request that promotion on transfer would be forthcoming. In Moore's view, 'this was impossible to concede as of right and such applications were withdrawn.' Clark headed a committee to examine applications for positions in government departments as well as the courts' service, 'where the Chief Justice has the right of choice in personnel uncontrolled by any Committee.' Thus Henry would have a large say in who worked in the Northern Courts.[87] Moreover, Moore said that 'a very large number of the applicants who were thought eligible were personally interviewed',[88] and while Henry is not explicitly mentioned here, in the light of Henry's work hitherto it is quite feasible that the Chief Justice met potential candidates himself.

Moore's memorandum also reveals some of the thinking behind appointments to the Northern Courts. Henry adopted a policy originated by Craig, that when candidates of equal merit were considered, the deciding qualification should be that the applicant was born in the Six Counties. Moore, apparently endorsing this proviso, wrote that since the inhabitants of the Six Counties had to bear the cost, 'it is right that they should have first claim on the employment it offers.'[89] One wonders if this was the real reason; did Craig perhaps believe that an 'Ulster' Judiciary would be better served by Ulstermen, or were northerners more 'loyal' than individuals from Dublin or London? Certainly, a survey of the backgrounds of some court officials implies that Craig's initiative was consistently carried out. The Assistant Registrars, R. McQuitty, J.G. Breakey and W. Horner, came from Belfast, County Antrim and Derry respectively. McQuitty had been associated with the County Courthouse in Belfast for about thirty years, and had been deputy to the Clerk of Crown and Peace. Breakey was educated at Coleraine and Queen's College, and worked in the Lord Chancellor's department in Dublin. Of the Assistant Chief clerks listed in Moore's Memorandum, all were Ulstermen; D. McGonigal and A.J. Weir came from Belfast, while F. Redmond hailed from Armagh.[90] Belfast's new Recorder, H.M. Thompson, was born in Cushendall.[91] Henry himself appointed J.M. Davies from Derry as Registrar, invited T. B. Wallace from Dromore, County Down, as Chief Clerk, and selected Barry Meglaughlin, a solicitor from Dungannon, as Taxing Master.[92] The Northern Judiciary was truly 'Northern' in all aspects.

However, it was left to Henry to clear up a nagging problem over staff appointments, which arose out of a Treasury requirement that the new officeholders should be retired on the usual Civil Service conditions, at ages from sixty to sixty-five years. Henry, 'in one of the visits to London which he was obliged to make', met Sir John Anderson at the Irish Office.[93] Henry impressed upon Anderson the necessity of getting experienced men for the new Judiciary, and warned that such people would not relinquish a position if they were aged, say, fifty-five years, and were to retire in seven years' time with a proportionately minor pension. It is not clear what form the meeting took thereafter, but it ended with Anderson's compliance, 'and all the first officials in the Courts on establishment were appointed for life or good behaviour.'[94]

As with courtroom accommodation, Henry was again at the forefront of affairs. His role was not to be a 'rubber-stamping' exercise, for he personally selected, in all probability interviewed and quite definitely had final say in the choice of candidates for the Northern Courts. Perhaps this aspect of Henry's work provides another reason why he was chosen as the first Lord Chief Justice; his knowledge of the circuits, judges, solicitors and court officials with whom he had come into contact during his many years as an advocate made Henry favourably placed to select the most able men. This issue saw further involvement by Craig, and Moore's notes convey the impression that Henry and Craig formed a cordial and close liaison. Moore refers to an instance when Henry suffered 'considerable anxiety' because no Order in Council had been passed fixing 1 October 1921 as the appointed day. When Henry informed Craig, the latter's subsequent contact with the Irish Office enabled him to report that, on 27 September, an Order had been issued by the King.[95] This affair caused Moore to remark: 'This was only one of the many occasions in which Sir James Craig's influence and immediate action led to a solution of a difficulty with the happiest results.'[96]

Henry was also engaged in solving quite ordinary and apparently mundane matters which arose in the early days of the Judiciary. He had to ensure that the necessary desks and furniture arrived for the new Court offices, and sent J.M. Davies to Dublin to select some of the forms used in the late High Court from which copies could be produced from the Stationery Office for use in the Northern Courts.[97] Henry had to make an agreement with the Council of Law Reporting in Ireland concerning their coverage and circulation of the Northern Courts' decisions, where it was decided that the Council's yearly publication should devote one-third of its space to reports of the High Court of Appeal, one-third to reports from Northern Ireland and one-third for Southern Ireland. Even so, this arrangement was 'provisional', and was made only 'after some delay'.[98] A similar point of issue occurred when the Belfast press refused to print the Law List or Legal Diary as an independent publication, as the press believed that the 'Law List' was a legal advertisement and accordingly should be paid for. Discussions on this subject eventually saw the Law List for the day published in the daily press,[99] with Moore commenting that, 'difficulties such as this, which ... after some trouble eventually overcome are incidental to the setting up of any new department, but they involve trouble and delay.'[100]

A large part of Henry's time was spent dealing with two vital aspects of the new Judiciary: ensuring an efficient and smooth-running judicial process, and fostering an amicable relationship between Bar and Bench. The former involved the modification of the Orders in Council which established the judiciary to meet the local circumstances, devising fair and adequate circuit arrangements, creating an appropriate Land Registry for Northern Ireland, and achieving a fair system of administering justice without overburdening jurors. This was all highly technical and complex, and just as he acquitted himself well in parliament when legal intricacies arose, Henry found himself no less at ease as Chief Justice.

One of Henry's early duties was to frame and consider Adaptation Orders relating to the Orders in Council which came into force on 27 September 1921, and in this Henry was assisted by J. S. Baxter, KC.[101] It was under an Adaptation Order that Henry founded the Rules Committee, which was designed to keep the rules under which the Northern courts functioned in touch with the requirements of both branches of the legal profession and the public. The Committee consisted of Judges and the President of the Northern Law Society, and Moore reported that the body 'has had many meetings.'[102]

Henry was unsuccessful in trying to resolve the difficulties surrounding the Land Registry of Northern Ireland. By July 1922, the Land Registry Office was not yet fully operational because documents relating to Northern Ireland had not been physically sorted out nor transferred from the late Central Office in Dublin to the new Central Office in Belfast. The problem was further aggravated by a dispute over the revenue of the staff, which included the question of whether or not the officials of the Land Registry were officers of the High Court and therefore pensionable. Henry held that these officers (who had all been nominated) were pensionable but the Lords Commissioners disagreed, and Moore noted that 'this may take some time for ultimate solution.'[103] This was the third occasion in which Henry and the Treasury had clashed; from the Memorandum, it appeared to be a confrontation between Henry's desire to achieve the best conditions for staff and get on with the job at hand, and the Treasury's inclination to observe rules and regulations regardless of circumstances.

Henry derived more satisfaction in creating a Commission to serve Belfast, making Circuit arrangements and contributing to the functioning of the High Court of Appeal for Ireland. As before, he drew on the assistance of Craig, but this area of Henry's work was to highlight even more the steady drain on Henry's physical resources. Moore outlined the background to the Belfast Commission established by Henry. Before 1921, Dublin was served by a Commission which dealt with crime in the County and City of Dublin and which met in Green Street Courthouse six times a year. Henry decided that a Commission should deal with crime in the City of Belfast,[104] and with Craig's assistance this Commission was obtained from the Imperial government. The Commission met four times a year, and by July 1922 had operated on three occasions, the first, appropriately, under Henry, the second under Moore, and the third under Andrews.[105] In March 1922, Henry and D. M. Wilson travelled the first Circuit of Northern Ireland, and a rota, involving the Lord Chief Justice and his two Lord Justices of Appeal, was prepared. Moore said that unless the Lord Justices took a share in the work of the Commission and Assizes, 'which strictly speaking they are not bound to do, there are not enough puisne judges to carry on the necessary work in Belfast.'[106] In the midst of this work Henry played his full part in the proceedings of the High Court of Appeal for Ireland. This Court consisted of the Lord Chancellor, the Lord Chief Justice of Ireland, and Denis Henry, and in 1922 Henry attended four sittings of this Court in Dublin.[107] In the first ten months of the Northern Judiciary, Henry travelled regularly to London, Dublin and various parts of Northern Ireland. In addition, innumerable problems fell to his attention. Recalling the busy schedule which Henry had faced as Attorney-General between 1919-1921, his early death through overwork is readily understandable.

In the early months of the Northern Courts, there was great demand placed on the jurors of Belfast, and Henry attempted to devise some scheme which would at least minimise the inconvenience caused to jurors. While jurors during the sitting of the courts were in constant attendance in Dublin and London, Henry and his colleagues arranged that jurors at the Belfast Commission would be sworn in before eleven o'clock, and any remaining jurors were discharged for the day.[108] The Committee on the Jury System of Northern Ireland, appointed in May 1923 and chaired by Lord Justice Andrews, referred in its report to the inequality of jury service in Belfast. The Committee said that in 1922, there were 6,296 names registered in the general Jurors' Book of the City of Belfast, of which 3,895 were required to serve, while 400 were summoned for the Winter Assizes which were held in County Antrim. If the jurors had been taken in proper rotation, only between one-half and two-thirds of the total number would have been needed, but the Sheriff, acting on existing legislation, was obliged to summon some jurors twice, while a large number escaped service entirely during 1922.[109] Whatever the shortcomings of the jury system, Moore observed that the Belfast juries had been attending 'very well', and that their verdicts were in keeping with the high standards expected of Belfast juries.[110]

A feature of Henry's Chief Justiceship was his achievement in fostering good relations with the Benchers of King's Inns, Dublin, and with the members of the Northern Bar. Before the Northern Judiciary was set up, all students for the Bar received their education and tuition under the auspices of the King's Inns, Dublin. After 1 October 1921, the Northern Judiciary would be responsible for its own students' academic welfare, but lack of funds, and the fact that there would be on average ten students a year, made the creation of a new Inn at Belfast impracticable. Moore was directed by Henry to attend a meeting of the Standing Committee of Benchers in Dublin, and as a result of their discussions the following conclusions were reached:

> the Lord Chief Justice of Ireland would call to the Bar of Southern Ireland all students called to the Bar in Northern Ireland, and the Lord Chief Justice of Northern Ireland would call to the Bar of Northern Ireland all students so called in Southern Ireland;[111] the Benchers of King's Inns would appoint and pay a professor of law to deliver lectures in Northern Ireland.[112]

Henry was grateful to Craig for his assistance in this matter, and more especially to Lord Justice Maloney, the Lord Chief Justice of Ireland, who gave Henry the services of trained civil servants in the Four Courts. In Moore's view, Maloney's help was indispensable: 'It was largely due to his influence that the working arrangement with the King's Inn was carried through.'[113]

The relationship between Bar and Bench was described as 'most cordial in a somewhat trying time of transition',[114] and Henry deserves credit for helping to bring this about. Henry and his other judges, along with the Attorney-General, gave the Northern Bar a gift of £100. In June 1922, in a 'novel departure', members of the Bar and Bench dined together 'as at a bar mess.' Afterwards, Henry and the other judges held a reception in his Chambers for those dining, and it was intended to continue this practice once a term.[115] Henry was a man of undoubted good humour, and it is quite conceivable that he intended to overcome any barriers or unease among his legal colleagues by an informal gathering, divorced from the traditional protocol of their profession.

As Lord Chief Justice Henry was inevitably involved in ruling on well publicised cases which reflected the turbulent times in which the Northern state functioned in its early years. The case of R (O'Hanlon) v. Governor of Belfast Prison in July 1922 saw the plaintiff, John James O'Hanlon, mount a challenge to the legality of the Special Powers Act; 'Were it not for the fact that this is the only Northern Ireland case on emergency law in this period, it is unlikely that this simplistic judgement would receive much attention.' James O'Hanlon, who had initially been detained under Regulation 23, and subsequently interned under Regulation 23 B, challenged his internment in Habeas Corpus proceedings before the Northern Ireland High Court on two grounds, i.e. by attacking the factual basis of any allegation against him by submitting an affidavit in which he denied involvement in any unlawful association or conspiracy, and by submitting that the introduction of internment under the Special Powers Act amounted to suspension of Habeas Corpus contrary to the terms of the 1920 Government of Ireland Act.[116]

O'Hanlon, a hotel proprietor from Portadown, had been arrested at his residence on 10 June 1922, and in a statement to the High Court the Inspector-General of the RUC, Charles Wickham, explained that 'Reliable information had come to the knowledge of the police authorities'. According to Wickham, this evidence, which was never disclosed, provided 'reasonable grounds' that O'Hanlon had committed an offence against the Regulations contained in the schedule to the Civil Authorities (Special Powers) Act (Northern Ireland) 1922, and he remarked that 'it would be prejudicial to the interests of justice and dangerous to the lives of those who supplied information' to divulge any further details. O'Hanlon's affidavit denied involvement in conspiracy and membership of any illegal body. He described how he had, like his father and grandfather before him, been a native of Portadown, spending over half of his forty-five years in the licensed trade, and owning, since April 1921, the Queens Hotel. A director of Portadown Gas Company for five years, O'Hanlon had held the Irish Chess Championship for the past nine years. The affidavit declared that 'Portadown has been for years peaceful and free from offences against law and order.'[117] T.J. Campbell, KC, defending, argued that the emergency legislation under which his client was detained left captivity to the uncontrolled will of the Attorney-General, which was 'a sweeping inroad on the old-established guarantees for the liberty of the subject.' Campbell described as 'rash' a statement by the Attorney-General, Richard Best, that there was a possibility that O'Hanlon would not recognise the court, and pointed out that when O'Hanlon had been arrested as having committed a crime, the intention was to try him, but on 8 July 1922, the eve of the trial, his status was changed from that of a person on remand to that of internee.[118]

In the light of Henry's attitudes as Attorney-General, his ruling on the O'Hanlon case was unsurprisingly supportive of the workings of the emergency law, and his judgement was delivered in his succinct direct way. The factual basis of the plaintiff's claim was briefly dismissed, for in Henry's words, 'The only question the court has to decide in an application of this kind is whether at the moment the matter comes before us O'Hanlon is legally held. We have nothing to do with the consideration of whether there is any evidence against him.' The Lord Chief Justice said that 'We simply have to say whether the two orders (Detention Order and Internment Order) which have been put before us as a reason for his being held comply with the law'. Accordingly, Henry ruled that the documents submitted by the Attorney-General complied with the law and there was sufficient authority for O'Hanlon to be held so long as the Executive desired. On legal issues, the ruling went on: 'This internment order is a modification of orders made in England almost every day by the Home Secretary there during the duration of the war dealing with persons of hostile origin or hostile association. The House of Lords in Halliday's case decided that the Home Secretary had power to make such orders, and that the Court was prevented from interfering with them. We decide that…the regulations are not *ultra vires*.'[119] In a highly critical editorial, the *Irish News* described James O'Hanlon as a respected citizen who had all his life believed in the constitutional way of procuring redress: he had been 'kidnapped in the name of the law'. The newspaper also questioned Henry's judgement, rejecting the court's view that 'it was not in their province' to interfere in what the paper referred to as 'the Executive's innocent victim'. In a clear reference to Henry, the *Irish News* argued that a Judge 'less careful of the feelings of the Executive' would make it plain that, in refusing O'Hanlon's application he was doing so because the machinery he was there to work was so ingeniously contrived by Sir James Craig's 'fair administration' that that left him no option but to bang in his face the door of the King's Courts to which all are asked to go who desire justice and the redress of wrongs.[120]

One of the most documented cases on which Henry had to deliberate was the Cushendall ambush of 23 June 1923 (the day after the assassination of Sir Henry Wilson), in which three Catholic youths were killed, allegedly without justification, by members of the 'A' Specials. According to the Police Report of the time, an attempted ambush on a combined British Army and Police patrol resulted in the death of three IRA men: John Gore, who had been interned in 1921; Patrick Hill; and James McAllister. The Report stated that a police car in the centre of Cushendall had been fired on, and that 'All arms and identities were removed from the killed and wounded by women'.[121] A heated letter from Joseph Devlin to Winston Churchill, Colonial Secretary, on 18 July, suggested quite a different version of events, and undoubtedly contributed to the subsequent independent inquiry which followed. Devlin promised to raise in parliament 'The question of wilful murder' which, he said, demanded sworn inquiry by an impartial commissioner. James McAllister, he said, was in a military tender three miles from the ambush, having been arrested while he cycled home. John Hill and John Gore, aged twenty and twenty-two respectively, hid in a shop in Cushendall when shooting began. Gore, an ex-soldier who had served in a Scottish regiment and had recently crossed to Ireland from Paisley, surrendered, and was shot dead. McAllister, according to Devlin, was being beaten by Specials, during the course of which a soldier said, 'If you have any humanity, and you want to kill him, shoot him at once'. A Special placed a revolver in McAllister's mouth, and fired. John Gore's brother, Patrick, was allegedly only saved from death by a local Special, who shouted, 'You shot his brother. Isn't that enough?' Devlin noted that the inquest had been held in Ballycastle, not Cushendall, and remarked that 'no evidence was admitted except as to the cause of death'. Devlin rounded on the government of Sir James Craig in his scathing conclusion; 'The state of terrorism which exists in the Cushendall district, consequent upon the murder, constitutes the gravest possible indictment of the system of tyranny, outrage, and intimidation which is in operation under and with the connivance of the Northern Government.'[122]

In a correspondence with Churchill on 20 July, Craig said that while he had no objection to an inquiry, 'judicial or otherwise', his Military Advisor, General Solly-Flood, was quite satisfied that a cleverly arranged ambush had been prepared in Cushendall, 'and that in defeating it the Specials and Military had acted with propriety and discretion'. Craig then gave a personal observation in which many Northern Nationalists would have found little credence, when he said, 'Moreover, as a better feeling now exists between all parties, and the incident occurred a considerable time ago, an enquiry of any sort will only revive bitterness and recriminations, while it certainly can do no good.'[123]

The involvement of British troops in the Cushendall incident prompted the British government to hold a judicial enquiry, and Churchill informed Craig that the proceedings would be conducted by F.T. Barrington-Ward, the Recorder of Hythe in Kent, a move which offered 'the best prospects of success and the least chance of friction by an English barrister of note.'[124] Barrington-Ward's inquiry was held in private, and in his report to the British government on 9 September 1922, Ward rejected the evidence of Specials and British soldiers that they had fired and killed in self-defence; 'My conclusion is that no one except the police and military even fired at all … I am unable to accept the evidence of the Special Constabulary from Ballymena. I am satisfied that they did not tell me all they knew about the circumstances in which three men died, and in view of the reports made by the military officers at the time and the evidence given by them before me, I do not believe that none of the police entered any of the houses.'[125]

Churchill, accepting Barrington-Ward's verdict on the killings, sent Craig a copy of the report on 12 October 1922, urging action against the Specials involved. Instead, the Northern government appointed J. R. Moorhead, the Chief Crown Solicitor to re-interview the witnesses, after which their own report rejected Barrington-Ward's conclusions and vindicated the actions of the Specials.[126] Moorhead's comment on the course of his investigation is indicative of the atmosphere of the time, as he recorded, 'I find on the part of many of the civilian witnesses a sentiment distinctly hostile to the Special Constabulary, and I would think it probable that the Special Constabulary might entertain a similar sentiment in the opposite direction.'[127] Certainly Richard Best, Attorney-General of Northern Ireland, left no doubt about his thoughts on the affair, rejecting Ward's findings on the grounds that they are 'largely based on the conclusion that no one except the police and military even fired at all on the occasion in question, and his report throughout hinges on that conclusion.' He went on: 'to anyone with experience of Irish witnesses there is nothing extraordinary in the number of civilians from a place like Cushendall, dominated up to recently by the IRA, coming forward to testify falsely against the Crown forces…any statements made by the people of Cushendall should be received with the greatest caution.'[128] The British government acceded to Craig's request not to publish Barrington-Ward's report lest it should embitter local feeling, 'now that normal conditions have been restored.'[129]

On 1 November 1923, the High Court of Justice in Northern Ireland, King's Bench Division, heard Denis Henry deliver judgement on claims for compensation arising out of the Cushendall shootings. The parents of John Gore, John Hill and James McAllister each claimed the sum of £2,000 in compensation, while Daniel O'Loan and John McCollum, each from Cushendall, claimed £1,000 and £250 respectively. Edward Sullivan Murphy, KC, who represented Antrim County Council,[130] had a practice in Dublin, and his father, Mr Joseph Murphy, had been the Queen's Bench Judge who had prosecuted the Phoenix Park murderers in 1882.[131] He questioned the reliability of the testimony from Cushendall residents, pointing to a key contradiction between the evidence of security forces and local people; namely, that while the latter said they had never heard of Sinn Fein activity in their area, the military swore that there were twenty to fifty men involved in the ambush. For the claimants, T.J. Campbell remarked on the statements from two Army officers from England and two members of the Specials, and claimed that 'not one of them knew the least thing about the crimes or had a particle of knowledge as to how the men met their death.' Campbell described the fact that Barrington-Ward had examined people who had not been called before the court as 'a most extraordinary fact – the most sinister fact in the case.' He challenged the military account that James McAllister was shot trying to escape from a lorry. With eleven security personnel present, he said, 'The suggestion of the escaping prisoner was only the effect of a fantastic imagination trying to account for his death.' Campbell concluded; 'The victims were the victims of ungovernable passion on the part of their attackers...reference to the deplorable murder of Sir Henry Wilson also illustrates that fact.'[132]

In his judgement, Henry referred to the 'extraordinary conflict of testimony' in statements made by witnesses for the plaintiffs. Accepting the evidence made by the British officers who had accompanied the Specials, and whose testimony corroborated that of the Specials, Henry agreed that the security forces had been fired on. He rejected the claims for compensation, and found that the deaths arose out of unlawful assembly. Henry was impressed by the military background of the Army officers who testified, commenting on the fact that the Major in charge of the party had been awarded the D.S.O., had had over twenty years' service and served through the Great War. 'It is perfectly clear', he said, 'that there was a considerable amount of shooting in the town that night, and whenever the forces of the Crown are attacked in that way, it becomes a very dangerous matter for any person to be about in the streets.' While sympathising with the relatives of the bereaved men, Henry rounded off his judgement thus: 'There were three responsible officers of the military in charge, three experienced officers. There were a lot of military there; there were two sergeants in charge of the police. They have given their evidence, and the onus is, as I said before, upon the applicants. I am not satisfied that that onus has been discharged and accordingly I refuse the application.'[133]

Henry enjoyed some rare yet pleasant diversions from the intensity of his work as Lord Chief Justice. In October 1923, Lord Carson paid a much publicised visit to the north, and the enclosed photograph, reproduced in this book, of the house party at Stormont Castle, attended by, among others, Henry and his wife, Sir James and Lady Craig, and Lord and Lady Carson, confirms the intimacy and esteem that Henry had with the leading figures of Ulster Unionism at that time. Indeed, with the separation of the Executive and Judiciary after 1921, it could only be at such an informal gathering that Henry could possibly be photographed with the Premier, Sir James Craig. Later, Carson addressed the Ulster Unionist Council at the YMCA building in Belfast, and in a wide-ranging speech, much of which was a eulogy to Ulster's stance against Home Rule, he devoted some time to the workings of the new Judiciary in Northern Ireland. He told his audience that he regarded 'the administration of justice as the basis of all society. If you can't have justice administered without fear or favour to any party ... you have no basis of liberty, and I do not think people sufficiently reflect that the whole question of liberty depends upon the administration of the law.' One wonders if the excitable audience viewed Carson's words as a warning about the workings of the new state, a piece of advice perhaps, or simply an observation from someone who had made his mark in the legal world. In what could be taken as an implied reference to Henry, Carson said that the most impressive aspect of 'your young Government' had been the work of those who had to carry out the decrees of the Courts; 'You have had the good fortune of having judges ... all of whom seem to me to have set out with the one single object – that no matter who the person brought before them is, be he on one side of politics or one side of religion or the other, he shall find in your courts absolute truth.'[134]

In October 1924, Lord Londonderry, the Minister for Education, raised in cabinet the possibility of Denis Henry being one of four nominations to the Senate at the Queen's University, Belfast, for which they would serve for a period of five years.[135] As a result, Henry received on 8 November a letter from Col. Spender, Craig's secretary, informing him that he had communicated with the Governor of Northern Ireland 'who is pleased to nominate you as one of the government's representatives of the Senate at Queen's University. I am to express the hope of the Government that you may see your way to accept this appointment'.[136] Henry, writing from his address at 12 Windsor Avenue, Belfast, duly accepted three days later. Incidentally, the other three nominations were Charles McLorinan, LLD, Belfast; Maxwell Scott Moore, JP, Derry, and Mrs J.C. White, Craigavad House, County Down.[137]

The early years of the Northern Judiciary were especially busy and trying for Henry. All aspects of the judicial machine fell to Henry for his attention, and as this chapter has witnessed the variety and degree of problems which Henry encountered were quite formidable. The office of Chief Justice seemed as much a test of character as of legal acumen, for Henry had to deal with many people: members of the Bar, judges, his southern counterparts, Council officials, Treasury officials, the Premier – the list is an extensive and all embracing one. Decisions had to be taken, advice sought, and meetings were frequent. In studying Moore's Memorandum, two obstacles emerged for Henry:

the lack of time and, as a corollary, the need to settle for compromises, rather than solutions. Courtroom accommodation is one issue which encapsulates both these themes most clearly, which leads to the question, how successful was Henry as Chief Justice? In many ways he acquitted himself well. His greatest achievement was in seeing that the Northern Judiciary functioned at a time when circumstances seemed to collaborate against this. Henry worked hard, and gave a lead. He personally met individuals to persuade them to co-operate, or to alter a ruling which he believed to be inhibiting the work of the Judiciary. Henry chose capable deputies, and personally interviewed new recruits. Moreover, his concern about such items as pensions for court officials, and his willingness to relax the atmosphere between Bench and Bar, reveal his deep personal interest in the people with whom he associated. Sir James Henry held that his father died through overwork, by taking on the problems of others and by trying to do too much. Sir James recalled meeting his father at the Courts in Belfast, and of how his father seemed to know everyone who passed them by. In the circumstances of the time, Sir James believed that confidence was needed by all those involved in the new Judiciary, and the feeling that the legal process could be got off the ground and could succeed was conveyed clearly by his father.[138] As Chief Justice, Henry was truly in demand, and some contemporary cabinet documents indicate this. When, in June 1922, the Lord Lieutenant, Fitz Alan, informed the Northern government that he would be going abroad for some months, Henry was mentioned as an individual who could act as Royal Commission in his absence.[139] Henry was also one of the chief witnesses before the departmental inquiry into the jury service in 1923, and his views clearly carried some weight and influenced the deliberations of the Committee.[140] In April 1925, Henry was consulted over nominations for the Pensions Appeal Tribunal.[141]

In 1922, Moore could claim that the Northern Judiciary was working quite adequately: 'the main work has been successfully achieved, the various parts of a great new legal machine have been assembled, and it is now running smoothly.'[142] Henry, while concurring with this sentiment, deprecated the deficiencies in courtroom facilities,[143] and lamented the absence of a Law Library for Bench and Bar, since the Queen's University Library facilities were a mere stopgap.[144] Herein lay a dilemma for the new judiciary; quick solutions to problems were needed, and some of the solutions just did not exist during Henry's tenure of office. For example, a proper courthouse for the Supreme Court takes time to build. However, Henry contributed to the assembling of a judicial machine, at a time when the existence of the State was being questioned. The machine was far from perfect, for it stuttered somewhat, and had to be pushed a little to make it go. But go it did – and at the time, that was all that mattered.

It is worth concluding this chapter by reflecting on an interesting footnote to Moore's Memorandum. Lord Justice Moore was one of two Lord Justices of Appeal in the Northern Judiciary, and his Memorandum relates to the period 1 October 1921 to 31 July 1922, and was made available to the public in PRONI in 1976. However, several letters attached to the Memorandum indicate that Moore wished to have its contents published, and the ensuing debate between Moore and the other branches of the Northern government implies a confused and perhaps uneasy relationship, as least regarding this matter. On 9 October 1922, Moore wrote to Sir James Craig about the Memorandum, and the letter is quoted thus:

Dear James

The Courts by being a Reserved Service do not report to anyone. But I thought it would assist the Northern situation if a statement were published showing the enormous amount of work in every direction done since this time last year in setting up the Courts, appointments, Circuits, as well as being of historical interest. I accordingly drew such a statement up; the C J warmly approved of the idea, but he is not to be asked to read it till it is in type. Dawson Bates was anxious to publish it as a Home Office document, but could not do so without leave from Finance, who told him to get an estimate, and said if he (Dawson) thought it useful, it would be all right. He got an estimate for £27. Now he writes me he cannot print it unless he first submits it to Pollock. I will not agree to any memo criticised or approved by any Minister ... and I have asked for its return. I would have naturally great pleasure in sending it to you and anything you wanted in or out, we would never fall out about. I do want it published to show the English and Scottish Bar that we are quite up to date with them here, and as a record of honest work to show the Northern Public what we have done, and all is running smoothly. If you will approve of its going to a government printer, will you tell Spender to give Newtown Anderson's instructions, and I will undertake it will not go further till you have seen proof.'[145]

There followed a correspondence between 11 October and 30 December 1922. A letter from A.P. Magill to Col. Spender, Craig's secretary, stated that the Minister of Home Affairs had studied the Memorandum, approved it, and assumed that it would be printed.[146] However, ten days later, on 14 November, Spender informed Magill that after a conversation between Craig and Henry, it was decided that the Memorandum should not be published.[147] On 28 November 1922, Spender contacted Henry, and reminded the Chief Justice that he and Craig had agreed 'that publication was, on the whole, inadvisable, and said that you would inform Lord Justice Moore accordingly.' It seemed that Moore was still pressing the minister of Home Affairs to have the Memorandum made public.[148]

A study of Moore's Memorandum makes it difficult to see why his observations on the early days of the Northern Judiciary should be withheld from the public for so long. Moore wanted publication, and judging from his letter he seemed to resent any restraint on his wishes, especially as he regarded the first ten months of the Judiciary as creditable and praiseworthy. Henry either consented to or gave Moore the impression of acquiescence in view of his intentions to publish – yet the Chief Justice changed his mind after meeting Craig.

Conclusions on the life
of Denis Henry

I N POOR HEALTH DURING THE summer recess of 1925, Henry went to Harrogate to seek medical advice, and shortly after his return to Belfast, took a severe seizure on Tuesday, 29 September. During his illness Henry was attended by two specialists, Dr Malcolm Brice Smyth and Dr MacIlwaine,[1] and was ministered to by Father Richard, Rector, Ardoyne, and Canon McDonnell, PP, St. Brigid's.[2] Denis Henry died on Thursday, 1 October 1925, at his home, 'Lisvarna', in Windsor Avenue.[3] He was sixty-one. He died on the anniversary of his wedding day, and on the same date on which the Northern Judiciary came into being in 1921. The funeral was held in private on Saturday, mass celebrated at Henry's home by his Jesuit brother, William (Thomas, who had joined the Marists, had predeceased Denis some years before), followed by burial at the family plot in Straw Cemetery in Draperstown. The chief mourners were Denis' sons, James Holmes and Denis Valentine; his brother, Alexander Patterson; his brothers-in-law, Edward Sullivan Murphy, KC, Harold Murphy, William Gage and Val Holmes; and Conolly Gage, son of William.[4] E.S. Murphy, of course, who had appeared in the Cushendall ambush case, went on to become an Appeal Court judge in the 1940s. E.S. Murphy's wife and Denis Henry's wife were sisters, being daughters of Lord Justice Holmes. William Charles Gage had been a long-standing family friend, previously named as an executor of Henry's will. William's son, Conolly, who was Denis Henry's nephew by marriage, followed his uncle's footsteps both in law and politics, entering Inner Temple in 1930, and later becoming M.P. for South Belfast between 1945 and 1952. Conolly Hugh Gage became Recorder of Saffron Waldon and Maldon in the 1950s, a County Court judge between 1958 to 1971, then a Circuit judge after 1972.[5]

The demise of Northern Ireland's first Lord Chief Justice was widely commented upon in the local and national press, by leading politicians and legal contemporaries, especially since very few outside Henry's immediate family circle knew that he had been ill, ensuring that his death 'came as a shock to all sections of the Belfast community.' The *Irish News*, surveying what it described as the 'remarkable career' of 'an eminent Catholic Unionist', described Henry as 'one of the ablest lawyers and advocates of his day at the Irish Bar.' The newspaper's generous tributes were tempered somewhat by a hint of criticism about Henry's Unionism, implying that, 'with virtually all Catholic members of the Bar' Home Rulers, a similar route by Henry would have confronted him with many rivals for the 'plums of the profession' when the Liberals were in power. 'As a Catholic Unionist', wrote the *Irish News,* 'in accordance with traditional policy, he was certain of securing the favours at the disposal of Tory insiders ... and he calculated wisely.' The *Irish News* was more generous of Henry's handling of controversial legal matters as Chief Justice, remarking that he had 'justified the Northern government's selection by his conduct of cases on the judicial bench', concluding that Henry was, 'on the whole, a fair-minded judge; personally, he was an upright citizen, a genial member of the community, highly esteemed by his friends. One of a notable Catholic family, he was sincerely attached to the faith of his fathers. He played an important, though not a great, part in the life of this country for the better part of twenty years.'[6] The *Times* praised Henry's tenure as Lord Chief Justice, stating that while many important cases had come before the High Court of Northern Ireland and some had been ultimately taken to appeal in the House of Lords, in no instance was any decision disturbed.[7] For the *Londonderry Sentinel,* Henry's death meant that 'Ulster loses a brilliant Ulsterman, the Northern Bench a distinguished lawyer, and the Northern Government a wise and tactful helper.'[8] The *Irish Law Times and Solicitors' Journal* commented that 'It is probably accurate to say that as a craftsman in the profession Henry had no superior.'[9]

Henry's work as Chief Justice during the troubled years of 1921 to 1925 was fully appreciated by Lord Carson and Sir James Craig. Carson revealed that he had 'read with the closest attention every judgement by Sir Denis Henry', and claimed that the Northern Judiciary 'was fortunate to start under the guidance of that great and eminent judge.'[10] Craig, who had learned of Henry's death on his way to Belfast for the meeting of the Northern Parliament, reiterated Carson's views on Henry's contribution to the establishment of 'our judiciary.' The Prime Minister's reference to the recent 'friendly correspondence' which he and his wife had had with Sir Denis and Lady Henry suggests that the successful collaboration between the two men during the early months of the Judiciary owed more to a close relationship than a formal liaison between premier and Law Officer.[11] Indeed, shortly after her husband's death, Lady Henry wrote to Lady Craig, saying that she knew no man 'for whom Denis had a greater regard, a more true affection, and a more profound admiration than your husband.' One of Craig's biographers and staunchest defenders presents this episode as 'another example of many that might be given' of Craig's 'amiable relations with his Roman Catholic countrymen. Henry, who had incurred harsh criticism from some of his co-religionists on accepting the office of Lord Chief Justice, was a faithful friend who worked for the Six Counties, as Craig wished all Ulstermen to work, in the belief that it was only by co-operation there that they could hope eventually for co-operation elsewhere.'[12]

Members of the legal profession were united both in their grief at Henry's passing and in their admiration of him as an advocate and a man. Sir John Ross, the last Lord Chancellor of Ireland, who had sworn in Henry as Lord Chief Justice in Portrush barely five years before, wrote that 'the late Sir Denis Henry was one of the finest types the North of Ireland has ever produced.'[13] In his contemporary study on the Supreme Court of Judicature of Northern Ireland, which appeared in 1926, George Hill Smith, KC, described how Henry's death on 1 October 1925 coincided with one of the days fixed for the Vacation Judge to sit and hear pressing Motions, whereupon the Members of the Bar and Solicitors engaged in cases went up to the Court House and were 'startled' by being told of the death of the Chief Justice. Lord Justice Moore entered the Appeal Court, and 'in trembling tone of voice' adjourned the Court and directed the Offices be closed till after the funeral.[14] The regrets of each branch of the legal profession were aired at a meeting of the Court House on 26 October. Moore recalled how he and Henry were contemporaries for nearly forty years at the Bar, in Parliament and on the Bench. As a lawyer, he regarded Henry as 'perhaps at his greatest in his knowledge of the Statute Law.' While Queen's University had had many distinguished graduates, Moore believed that 'Denis Henry of Draperstown was one of the most brilliant of her sons'. Describing Henry as 'essentially a shy man', who nonetheless was 'fully equipped' for legal battle, Moore said that he would always be remembered as 'the Founder of this Supreme Court – the Court of his own creation which he loved to his death.'[15]

Richard Best, Attorney-General, recollected the personality of Henry, remarking that he 'received nothing but kindness' from him. One 'little act of kindness' which he recalled occurred when Henry granted Best 'the very high honour' of accompanying him to Portrush where he was to be sworn in by Sir John Ross. Henry, he said, 'was the friend of everyone and never forgot his friends.'[16]

While Denis Henry's political and religious outlook make him stand out in contemporary Ulster politics, his allegiance to the Unionist cause is less remarkable in the context of his background, education and nature of politics in the last two decades of the nineteenth century. The Henry family had prospered in Draperstown under the Union, and while Liberal in outlook, failed to follow Gladstone's sudden conversion to Home Rule. In the circumstances of 1886, Denis Henry's endorsement of Unionism is unremarkable, given the political cleavage that Home Rule caused in Ulster politics. Henry's education clearly underpinned his Unionism, with the conservative influences of the Jesuits at Mount St. Mary's fortifying his politics in his formative years. His English public school education and his Queen's experiences, where he excelled in his legal studies, undoubtedly gave Henry a wider perspective on Ulster politics. Henry's support for the Union has been traced back as far as the introduction of the 1886 Home Rule Bill when he was in his early twenties and creating the potential for a successful legal carer. There can be little doubt that Henry's commitment to the Union was deeply held some time before he first stood as a Unionist candidate in North Tyrone in 1906. It is worth recalling that on the occasion of his death, the *Times* described Henry as a 'staunch Unionist', who had 'in the long-drawn struggle against Gladstonian Home Rule played a notable part, speaking with great effect at numerous meetings in England and Scotland.'[17] Henry's appearance on E.T. Herdman's platform in the 1895 election in East Donegal indicates consistency as well as commitment. Of greater significance was Henry's attendance as a Unionist delegate at the inaugural meeting of the Ulster Unionist Council on 3 March 1905, which indicated that he was fully accepted by those who would be directing the affairs of the Unionist Party in years to come.[18] In the light of this evidence, Henry's candidature in North Tyrone in the following year seems more understandable.

Denis Henry's participation in parliamentary elections in North Tyrone (1906–1907) and South Derry (1916 and 1918) gives an insight into the reaction he received from contemporary Unionists and Nationalists, provides an illustration of his attitude to the Union, and contributes to our knowledge of his character and personality. Nationalist predictions during the 1906 North Tyrone election that Henry's religion would result in rejection by Orangemen proved misplaced, for Henry not only received wholehearted support from the Orange Order throughout the campaign, but a rapport was established which Henry was to retain during his political career. Henry was unanimously selected in Kilrea Orange Hall to contest South Derry in December 1918, and the Grandmaster of the Orangemen of the constituency appeared on his platform as well. W. S. Armour described how, while Unionists in North Antrim were taken in their motor cars 'to save the empire and keep out a Papish', in South Derry 'they would have had, with their Orange brethren, to vote for Denis Henry – one of the Pope's brigade. It is a topsy-turvey world in truth.'[19] In 1907, the Ulster Liberal Unionist Association passed a resolution supporting Henry in North Tyrone, while Carson endorsed his candidature in South Derry in 1918. When Henry's second defeat in North Tyrone prompted the *Irish News* to speculate on his future relationship with Unionists, the Unionist women of North Tyrone presented Henry with an inscribed silver tray in recognition of his 'two spirited contests' in the constituency 'on behalf of the Union.' The *Londonderry Sentinel* noted how on one occasion Henry went to the Guildhall in Derry to speak at an election meeting in support of his close friend, Sir John Ross. The meeting was in progress when Henry arrived, but no sooner was he recognised on entering the platform than the entire audience rose in a body and cheered him for several minutes. 'I was greatly shaken', Henry told a friend afterwards. 'there was a packed gathering of Orangemen, making the hall ring with cheers for me, a Catholic.'[20] Strangely, while it was appropriate that Henry should win his first parliamentary seat in South Derry in 1916, his victory in his native constituency was both paradoxical and unique. The uniqueness of the occasion comes from the fact that Henry's success represented the first instance in the twentieth century in which a Catholic Unionist successfully contested an Ulster constituency, with this contest being the first Westminster election in Ireland since the Easter Rising. The paradox lies in the circumstances surrounding Henry's nomination, for while Henry was clearly very popular among Unionists, it was by no means certain that he would win the three-way contest involving Reid and Chichester. Only Reid's withdrawal enabled Henry to defeat Chichester by 17 votes to 10 in the final count.

The reaction of Nationalists to Denis Henry's election appearances could not have provided a greater contrast to the welcome which he received from Unionists. There was open scepticism about Henry's support of Herdman in 1895, as Henry was regarded as a peculiarity who would perhaps disappear from politics never to be seen again. This attitude was replaced by hostility, as Nationalists realised that Henry was presenting a serious candidature in North Tyrone in 1906 and 1907. The paradox of the South Derry success of 1916 can be taken further when one surveys the shifting Nationalist posture. In a spirit of toleration, one Catholic clergyman in Kilrea declared that Catholics could feel confident that 'the interests of our religion' would be supported by Denis Henry, while Father Patrick Convery, Parish Priest of St. Paul's, Belfast, sent a congratulatory telegram to the new Member for South Derry. Convery, a native of Maghera, County Derry, close to Draperstown, had been a strong Nationalist and Parnellite, a President of the Belfast Branch of the National League, and was later eulogised by Alice Milligan, the Protestant Nationalist poetess.[21] By 1918 Henry's stance was so familiar to Nationalists that his successful defence of South Derry passed without comment. Indeed Henry's campaign was only sparsely reported outside of the immediate locality, and only the *Coleraine Chronicle* and *Northern Constitution* provided any details on the election of the last Catholic Unionist MP in Ulster politics.

Henry's strong defence of the Union undoubtedly contributed to his popularity among Ulster Unionists. Many years after Henry's death, a contributor to the *Impartial Reporter* described a speech in Strabane in which Henry 'implored the British government' to cede Ulster to Germany in 'preference to betrayal of the North's position in the United Kingdom'.[22] However, Henry's credibility as a Catholic Unionist was not only helped by the fact that he had declared his political allegiance early in his career, but also by a combination of personal charm, ability to mix with others of various political outlooks, and by the fact that he was one of the outstanding legal lights in the Irish Bar. Henry's 'eccentric' political views were clearly 'forgiven' by the unanimous acclaim which his personality and legal ability commanded. T.J. Campbell, for example, with his strong Belfast Nationalist background, was wholehearted in his praise for Henry both as a person and as a lawyer. W.E. Wylie refused to let his political differences with Henry over government policy during the Anglo-Irish War cloud his recollections of Henry's warmth and wit as Father of the North-West Circuit.

The Circuit embraced a proportion of the country which does an injustice to the term 'North-West', as it covered County Westmeath, Cavan, Tyrone, Londonderry and Derry City; County Longford, Fermanagh and Donegal.[23] The intimacy of the Circuit is reinforced by the fact that, late in his political and legal career, Henry was associated with his brother, Alexander Patterson Henry, W.E. Wylie, Marcus Begley and Edward S. Murphy – all of whom served in the North-West Bar.[24] Henry's humour and affability with political opponents reflected not only his personality but is revealing of the manner with which Irish politics was conducted in the early years of the century. A chorus of boos and hisses directed at Henry during the 1907 North Tyrone by-election was interrupted by a female voice exhorting Henry to 'away and get a good Presbyterian wife !' When another heckler asked, 'What are you going to do for Ireland?', Henry replied, 'I am going to try and keep the disorderly elements in subjection'.[25] An amusing incident during Henry's narrow defeat by Dodd in North Tyrone the previous year sheds light, if it is to be believed, on the allocation of one of those vital votes. An elderly man was carried to the poll by a clergyman and some enthusiastic Nationalists. As he was to vote as an illiterate, the presiding officer informed him that there were two candidates, Dodd and Henry, and asked him for which he desired to vote. Much puzzled, the elderly man blustered out 'Henry', whereupon the Nationalists ran down the stairs in disgust and left him helpless in the booth. 'Then happened a strange thing; a number of Orangemen, arrayed in their sashes, carried him home with cheers and applause as a loyalist hero.'[26] The manner with which Henry accepted defeat in North Tyrone in 1906 and 1907 did him credit, especially since coming second best was something that he was unaccustomed to in his professional career. The *Londonderry Sentinel* referred to Henry's 'generosity' when hearing the news of his nine vote defeat to Dodd in 1906, since 'It was notorious that Mr. Dodd's return by a majority of 9 could have been upset on petition, but the defeated Unionist refused to move against a brother lawyer.'[27]

Henry's ability to socialise with individuals from all political backgrounds sustained his stance as a Catholic Unionist. His determination as both Father of the North-West Circuit and later as head of the Northern Judicature to break down barriers between legal men was widely known, and he was quite at ease in social situations. One correspondent for the *Irish Times* described 'a little speech' made by Henry at the inaugural dinner of the Dublin University Graduates' Association. While there had been 'considerable speaking' up to that point, 'and good speaking' too, it seems that the atmosphere was not fully congenial. However, Henry spoke 'for not more than five minutes, but in that time he succeeded in insulting every university and faculty represented in the hall! After that speech the complete success of the dinner was assured.'[28] The intimacy of the Irish Bar facilitated political differences, and Wylie's memoirs illustrate that it seemed to be a matter of great pride that lawyers could work together regardless of their personal political convictions. The brief references to Henry by Tim Healy and T.P. O'Connor are a case in point. Healy, who had won South Derry as a Parnellite in 1885, and who served in both the English and Irish Bar, recalled Henry warmly: 'Denis (at the time of his death) had a priest after sixty years.'[29] Healy noted that Henry represented the Nationalist M.P. for Galway North, Richard Hazleton, in 1915, indicating that the aftermath of the Home Rule crisis left relationships in the legal world unimpaired.[30] Healy felt at ease in discussing the Lloyd George partition scheme of 1916 with both Henry and Arthur Warren Samuels,[31] and described how, in September 1921, shortly after Henry's appointment as Lord Chief Justice, he met him on a sea crossing and debated the recent elections for the Northern Parliament. Henry, he said, told him that 'thousands of Catholics in Tyrone and Derry voted for the Tory', to which Healy replied, 'they must have been the A.O.H.', and Henry agreed.[32] The fact that Healy was able to sustain friendly relations with an old acquaintance of Henry's, Sir Edward Carson, reinforces the atmosphere of the Irish Bar. 'When I went to see Carson', wrote Healy, 'he was the same friendly fellow that he had always been, but would not budge an inch.'[33] Healy too, recalled how he represented Mrs Sheehy Skeffington during the Simon inquiry into her husband's death in 1916, commenting that 'The terms of reference of the inquiry restricted Simon', adding ambiguously, 'He had a colleague in Denis Henry to cope with.'[34] In a moving tribute to Henry, T.P. O'Connor, who had for many years been one of Redmond's closest friends in the Irish Party, observed that no matter how heated debates in parliament may have been, Henry and his contemporaries remained on friendly terms: 'They hated his politics, but did not – nobody could – hate the man'. Henry, he said, had been 'a somewhat unique type of Irish life; Catholic by descent and personality', his family had 'always belonged to the prosperous middle-class in Ulster', yet they 'shared none of the enthusiasm of their co-religionists, and it was in this realistic atmosphere that he was brought up.'[35] Maurice Healy, brother of Tim, provides an interesting contrast between Henry's fellow Catholic (Southern) Unionist, William Kenny, who fared less well in his personal relationships with political rivals; 'A Catholic Unionist was never a very popular figure in Ireland, and Kenny was heatedly disliked by the Irish Party, who never missed a chance of girding him in the House.'[36]

In his courtroom style, Henry combined a tall commanding figure with a quiet, unassuming yet effective style. T.P. O'Connor described Henry as 'a tall, stout, red-faced man with a mane of hair rising high above his head, and in later years very white.'[37] Edward Jones recalls how, in his youth, his father took him to Portrush on a courtesy call to Henry when he was Lord Chief Justice. Jones wrote later, 'I remember that Lady Henry was there and I also have a vivid recollection of Sir Denis who struck me as a great crag of a man.'[38] One correspondent commented on Henry's 'unique' courtroom manner; 'no matter how close and keen his cross-examination of a witness might be, he never bullied or hectored, but in his quiet, courteous, gentlemanly manner he brought out, nonetheless, what he wanted to bring out.'[39] This was illustrated effectively by Maurice Healy's reminiscences of the old Munster circuit. During the Anglo-Irish War, an English barrister in a Dublin court invited Attorney-General Henry to cross-examine a witness who had apparently provided a solid alibi for the accused. Healy describes the exchange which followed:

> Henry (very quietly): 'Where did you say you lived?'
> The witness repeated his address.
> Henry: 'How many doors from the prisoner's house?'
> Witness: 'Next door.'

At this point Henry sat down, and as Healy recounts, 'Denis knew perfectly well that the alibi witness had probably been taken through his story by his own friends a hundred times, and cross-examined each time. All that would be necessary to direct the jury's attention to the probable falsity of the story would be to draw attention to some link between the prisoner and the witness. Denis had done that.'[40]

While Henry's place as a Catholic Unionist ensures him a unique place in Ulster politics, in the wider context of contemporary Southern Unionism his political and religious outlook makes him appear quite unremarkable. In fact, there is some evidence to suggest that Denis Henry would have been quite at ease in the Southern Catholic Unionist tradition of the later nineteenth and early twentieth centuries. Henry would have been comfortable with the Southern Unionist philosophy of welcoming Catholics into their ranks 'to prove that the union was widely recognised as most beneficial to Ireland.'[41] Recent research indicates a correlation between Henry's background and that of Catholic Unionists in the South and West, who included landlords, soldiers and lawyers, 'and a fair number of resolute supporters of law and order, some of whom were instinctively conservative and others who were unimpressed by the case for Home Rule'. Or, as one Unionist pamphleteer put it, 'all the Irish Roman Catholic gentry, three-quarters of the Roman Catholic professional men, all the great Roman Catholic merchants and half of the domestic class.'[42] Writing a year after the defeat of the 1886 Home Rule Bill, the *Northern Whig* proclaimed that attachment to the Union was 'not confined to Protestants; it is shared by the most respectable Catholics.'[43] This view was echoed five years later by W.E.H. Lecky who, in a letter to the *Times,* wrote that he had never 'looked upon Home Rule as a question between Protestant and Catholic. It is a question between honesty and dishonesty, between loyalty and treason, between individual freedom and organised tyranny and outrage.'[44] Henry's Marist and Jesuit upbringing readily springs to mind when one considers the view that, while Catholic

Unionists 'may have deplored the way in which the Catholic clergy tended to identify Catholicism with Irish nationalism,' they could console themselves with the fact that, for the most part, the Catholic Church was a conservative force, upholding the status quo, defending property and existing order so long as the state abstained from attacking their ecclesiastical rights.'[45] Reference to Catholic Southern Unionists like William Kenny reinforces the similarity with Henry's political outlook and career. Born in Dublin in 1846, and privately educated, Kenny attended Trinity College, and was called to the Irish Bar in 1868, aged twenty-two, becoming a Queen's Counsel in 1885. Pushed into politics by the shock of the 1886 Home Rule Bill, Kenny became joint secretary of the Irish Branch of the Liberal Union, telling his colleagues that 'We are determined to show that Unionist Ireland is not represented by Ulster alone'.[46] Standing as a Liberal Unionist, Kenny won the St. Stephen's Green seat in Dublin in 1892.

In contrast to the acclaim which his legal work inspired, Denis Henry had a less happy time as Attorney-General for Ireland during the Anglo-Irish War. While the evidence indicates that Henry departed from Westminster in August 1921 with his personal reputation untarnished, he must have found many aspects of his work unsatisfactory. When he took the floor of the House to deal with the many contentious issues which inevitably came his way as Law Officer, it was often in the unaccustomed position of a defensive and ill-informed individual who lacked knowledge of the precise nature of events. His sparse and direct replies to probing questions about the activities of Crown forces or the implementation of emergency legislation contained an edge of terseness and at times barely concealed frustration at being unable to convey the assurance and conviction he normally carried in court. Moreover, Henry was to discover that while one could provide legalistic arguments and information in a calm, legalistic manner in the privacy of cabinet, it was to be quite another thing to defend government policy in public debate. Henry's reaction to the Derry riots, for example, was only one of several occasions in which he appeared out of touch with what was happening. While the frequent absences of the Chief Secretary, Hamar Greenwood, undoubtedly made Henry's life more difficult, there was an ironic sense in which this worked in his favour, as parliamentary critics and correspondents alike took a more sympathetic line towards Henry during debate, angrily drawing attention to the seldom present Greenwood. Here, too, Henry's personality stood him in good stead, for even in the atmosphere engendered by the Mountjoy hunger-strike, critics like T.P. O'Connor seemed to appeal to Henry on a personal level, almost distancing the beleaguered Attorney-General from government policy. One wonders if these M.P.s knew of Henry's consistently hard-line approach in cabinet to the prosecution of the Anglo-Irish War and his rejection of talks with Sinn Fein, would they have been so willing to give Henry the benefit of the doubt. The Patrick Casey affair reveals much about Henry's mood as well as the personal good fortune he enjoyed in the House. Members let Henry off lightly by failing to probe the *exact* circumstance of Casey's arrest; if he had fired on Crown forces, why was he himself not shot ? Was he found in possession of a weapon, and if not, what was the proof of his involvement ? Henry's comment that Crown forces did not get 'twenty-five hours' like Casey to prepare for their deaths left him open to the charge that an Irish Law Officer was placing the activities of the forces of law and order on the same level as the very lawbreakers whom they were empowered to apprehend. His words were indicative of the tiredness and strain which Henry was experiencing; after all, his life was in daily danger, as well as revealing Henry's personal bitterness at seeing the Ireland he knew, of freedom to move between the North-West Circuit and the Four Courts, being destroyed by the Republican campaign against the machinery of the state. T.P. O'Connor described how, when Henry 'held office' (presumably as Attorney-General and Lord Chief Justice), he made it a rule never to leave his house at night. Even during the day, he said, he kept to open and broad streets, where a possible assassin would have little chance of getting at him. Yet, as O'Connor notes, 'Henry went through this with a sort of solid and good-humoured composure.'[47] Mark Sturgis' scathing rebuke of September 1920 that 'the Attorney-General (Henry) sits in London afraid to set foot in Ireland' is contradicted by Maurice Healy and by Sturgis himself. According to his private diaries, Sturgis recorded how, in January 1921, Henry had to come to Ireland to give a judicial ruling on the delayed execution of Joseph Murphy, who had appealed against his sentence on the grounds that 'an admirable cross-examination was wrongly disallowed.'[48] Henry – while privately feeling that 'the proceedings were, notwithstanding, valid'[49] – arrived in Dublin on Sunday, 16 January, with Sturgis reassuringly 'having ordered car and escort to met him.' Staying with Sir Henry Wynne, Chief Crown Solicitor for Ireland,[50] Henry attended the proceedings at the Four Courts for several days, confiding to Sturgis that the 'Murphy case will go in our favour on law, his doubt being whether the Court will or not recommend mercy.'[51]

Denis Henry's appointment as the first Lord Chief Justice of Northern Ireland marked the final chapter on his legal career. The lack of contemporary surprise at the choice of Henry can be explained by his widespread reputation earned at the Irish Bar, his perceived ability to work well with people, as well as his determination to endorse controversial emergency legislation in private and in public. In retrospect it seems remarkable that the choice of a Catholic as the first Lord Chief Justice should pass virtually unnoticed by both Nationalists and Unionists alike. One plausible explanation for this is that in 1921 Northern Nationalists believed that the new state would be of short duration, while Unionists were preoccupied with the assembling and survival of the state and less interested in any 'propaganda' to be made from the appointment of a Catholic to one of the key posts in the administration. Indeed, the only attempt to claim credit for the choice of Henry came almost by accident in a lecture given by Dr H.S. Morrison, who had endorsed Henry's candidature in South Derry. Addressing the Woodvale and Falls

Womens' Unionist Association in November 1921, Morrison referred to the harmony which characterised South Derry politics since 1886 – 'clean, honest strenuous fighting, and no bitterness.' He told his audience that in the 1918 election in South Derry, Henry was selected by the Unionist Association, 'though probably half the delegates were Orangemen.' South Derry, said Morrison, happily integrated between Orange and Green, 'and if the Nationalists were willing they could map the routes for possession and dispense entirely with the police.'[52] Once appointed, Henry embraced the daunting schedule of work which inevitably awaited someone heading a new judiciary, and his qualities of hard work, knowledge of law and ability to work with people were admirably demonstrated. His response to controversies over the O'Hanlon case and Cushendall ambush were predictable in the light of his parliamentary record in defending emergency legislation and the action of Crown forces in difficult circumstances. Moreover, issues like courthouse accommodation, the choice of officials, interpretation of law and the procurement of a Bar Library all fell to Henry, and while some problems could never be completely resolved during his tenure of office, Henry's contribution in the early years of the Northern Judiciary was unmistakable.

It is a matter of supposition as to why, since the general election of December 1918, no Catholic has won a Westminster seat for the Ulster Unionists. Perhaps it was easier for Denis Henry to assert Catholic Unionism in the political circumstances of *his* time, and in an environment of an Irish Bar conducive to toleration of conflicting opinions. One advantage which Henry enjoyed was that not only did he declare his Unionism early in his life but also at a time when many followers of Gladstone were reassessing their loyalty to the Liberals over the introduction of the first Home Rule Bill of 1886. Bearing in mind the dramatic cleavage which Home Rule caused in both British and Irish politics, Henry's 'conversion' to Unionism was neither unique nor special. Moreover, Sir James Henry stressed that his father benefited from an early declaration for Unionism, was open and unequivocal, and while many might have disagreed with him, most people at least accepted his father as a Catholic Unionist. By 1921, Denis Henry was a well-known figure in Ulster politics, and his Catholic Unionism evoked little comment. Coupled with his affable personality and considerable legal ability, this goes some way to explain why his elevation to the position of Lord Chief Justice in August 1921 passed almost unnoticed. One wonders what the reaction in Ulster politics would have been if such a promotion had occurred, say, in the 1930s. It was more acceptable for Henry to make his Catholic Unionist stand in the 1880s, at a time of political flux and with a considerable strain of Catholic Unionism in the south of Ireland, for it is possible that the partitioning of Ireland after 1921 imposed a pressure on Catholics and Protestants to conform to their respective Nationalist and Unionist traditions with which they are so closely identified today. The bitterness of the Home Rule crisis, the atmosphere of disorder in Ireland after 1916, and the belief that the Northern State was impermanent combined to make it difficult for an Ulster Catholic to declare for Unionism and be accepted thus. When the Boundary Commission Report of 1925 (published several weeks after Henry's death) finally dashed this latter expectation, Ulster Nationalists displayed resentment or indifference to the workings of Northern Ireland. In these circumstances, the likelihood of a Catholic adopting a high profile Unionist stance in politics was remote. Occasionally, the issue of Catholic Unionists arose in the politics of Northern Ireland. In November 1959, Sir Clarence Graham, chairman of the Standing Committee of the Ulster Unionist Council, said that if a Catholic wanted to represent the Unionist cause in Westminster, it would be a matter for the local constituency association. Shortly afterwards, Sir George Clark, Grandmaster of the Grand Orange lodge of Ireland, remarked that it would be difficult to see 'how a Catholic, with the vast differences in our religious outlook, could be either acceptable as a member or bring himself unconditionally to support its ideals.'[53] The experiences of Louis Boyle in the 1960s are of relevance here. Boyle joined the Conservative and Unionist Association of Queen's University Belfast in 1965, and became its first Catholic president two years later. Shortly after helping to form the South Down Young Unionist Association, becoming its first vice-chairman, Boyle put his name forward as Unionist candidate for South Down in February 1969, only to find that the South Down Unionist Association had decided not to contest the election.[54] In a subsequent resignation statement, Boyle declared that the Unionist Party's sectarian foundations made Catholic membership difficult, writing that the party needed to break its links with the Orange Order, referring to the holding of Unionist meetings in Orange Halls, which, he said, 'no Catholic could in conscience attend if allowed.'[55] This marked a stark contrast with Denis Henry's electoral experiences. Patrick Shea, one of the few Catholics to rise to the position of Permanent Secretary in the Northern Ireland civil service, believed that after 1945 the Unionist government could have done more to win the trust of Catholics, but felt that events surrounding the formation of Northern Ireland were seared too deeply into the minds of those who held power for such a rapprochement to take place.[56] In a letter to the *Daily Telegraph* in April 1975, the leader of the Ulster Unionist Party, Harry West, wrote that after 'the Sinn Fein violence' of the 1920s, a career like Denis Henry's would be 'virtually impossible.'[57] Perhaps if Ulster Unionists had been less concerned with defending the new state in 1921, they might have examined the long-term implications of appointing several Catholics to positions of comparable importance to that of Henry's. Certainly, the absence of a Catholic Unionist M.P. in Ulster politics is a potent comment on the nature of politics in Northern Ireland since 1921.

ENDNOTES

Footnotes for Chapter 1:
'Early life and involvement in politics.'

1   *Irish News*, 13 July 1984.
2   Interview with Sir James Henry on 29 July 1979, in London.
3   A. J. O'Keeney *Looking Back on Ballinascreen* (Ballinascreen Historical Society, 1989)
4   *Irish News*, 13 July 1984.
5   LR1641: Will of James Henry and other family members (PRONI).
6   *Ibid.*
7   PRONI SCH655 / 1 / 1: Draperstown National School for Boys, 1870-1903 (PRONI).
8   *Irish News*, 13 July 1984.
9   E. Walsh *Famous Maghera Men* (c. 1970).
10 S. O' Ceallaigh *Gleanings from Ulster History* (Ballinascreen Historical Society, 1994), p47.
11 J. S. Curl *The Londonderry Plantation* (Phillimore, 1986), p198
12 S. O' Ceallaigh *op. cit.* p47
13 *Ibid.* p56
14 *Ibid.* p57
15 J. S. Curl *op. cit.* 223
16 *Ibid.* p226.
17 PRONI SCH655 / 1 / 1 : *op. cit.*
18 Mount St. Mary's College archives.
19 *Londonderry Sentinel*, 3 October 1925.
20 Interview with Sir James Henry on 29 July 1979, in London.
21 *Ibid.*
22 *Londonderry Sentinel*, 6 January 1906.
23 *Ibid.* 9 January 1906.
24 P. Buckland *Irish Unionism, 1885-1923* (Belfast, 1973), p59
25 J. Biggs-Davison and G. Chowdharay-Best *The Cross of St. Patrick: The Catholic Unionist Tradition in Ireland* (Kendal, 1984), p 290
26 LR1641 *op. cit.*
27 Interview with Sir James Henry on 29 July 1979, in London.
28 *Times,* 31 July 1895.
29 B. M. Walker *Parliamentary Election Results in Ireland, 1801-1921* (Dublin, 1978), p164.
30 *Derry Journal,* 29 July 1895.
31 *Ibid.* 29 July 1895.
32 *Ibid.* 29 July 1895.
33 *Ibid.* 29 July 1895.
34 *Ibid.* 29 July 1895.
35 *Ibid.* 29 July 1895.
36 *Ibid.* 12 July 1895.
37 *Ibid.* 19 July 1895.
38 *Ibid.* 26 July 1895.
39 *Londonderry Sentinel,* 3 October 1925.
40 *Irish Law Times and Solicitors' Journal,* 4 June 1898, p263.
41 *Derry Journal,* 9 December 1898.
42 *Ibid.* 9 December 1898.
43 *Ibid.* 8 December 1898.
44 *Ibid.* 12 December 1898.
45 *Ibid.* 12 December 1898.
46 B. M. Walker *op. cit.* p375-376.
47 *Londonderry Sentinel,* 9 March 1907.
48 *Ibid.* 9 March 1907.
49 B. M. Walker *op. cit.* Pp375-376.
50 *Irish News,* 3 January 1906.
51 *Northern Whig,* 22 December 1905.
52 *Ibid.* 28 December 1905.
53 *Derry Journal,* 3 January 1906.
54 *Irish News,* 9 January 1906.
55 *Ibid.* 9 January 1906.
56 *Londonderry Sentinel,* 2 January 1906.
57 *Ibid.* 2 January 1906.
58 *Ibid.* 4 January 1906.
59 *Ibid.* 2 January 1906.
60 *Derry Journal,* 5 January 1906.
61 *Londonderry Sentinel,* 2 January 1906.
62 *Ibid.* 6 January 1906.
63 *Ibid.* 6 January 1906.
64 *Ibid.* 9 January 1906.
65 *Ibid.* 6 January 1906.

66   *Ibid.* 2 January 1906.
67   *Ibid.* 2 January 1906.
68   *Ibid.* 6 January 1906.
69   *Derry Journal*, 3 January 1906.
70   *Londonderry Sentinel*, 6 January 1906.
71   *Ibid.* 6 January 1906.
72   *Ibid.* 2 January 1906.
73   *Ibid.* 13 January 1906.
74   *Ibid.* 6 January 1906.
75   *Ibid.* 9 January 1906.
76   *Ibid.* 4 January 1906.
77   *Derry Journal*, 10 January 1906.
78   *Ibid.* 19 January 1906.
79   *Londonderry Sentinel*, 13 January 1906.
80   *Derry Journal*, 17 January 1906.
81   *Ibid.* 12 January 1906.
82   *Londonderry Sentinel*, 11 January 1906.
83   *Derry Journal*, 17 January 1906.
84   *Londonderry Sentinel*, 13 January 1906.
85   *Ibid.* 11 January 1906.
86   *Derry Journal*, 22 January 1906.
87   *Londonderry Sentinel*, 23 January 1906.
88   *Ibid.* 23 January 1906.
89   *Ibid.* 23 January 1906.
90   *Derry Journal*, 22 January 1906.
91   *Londonderry Sentinel*, 23 January 1906.
92   *Irish News*, 23 January 1906.
93   D 2298/16/1: Letters held by Wilson and Simms, solicitors, Strabane (PRONI).
94   *Londonderry Sentinel*, 7 March 1907.
95   *Ibid.* 23 January 1906.
96   *Ibid.* 23 January 1906.
97   *Ibid.* 23 January 1906.
98   *Ibid.* 28 February 1907.
99   *Ibid.* 9 March 1907.
100 *Ibid.* 28 February 1907.
101 *Times*, 1 March 1907.
102 *Irish News*, 28 February 1907.
103 *Ibid.* 28 February 1907.
104 *Derry Journal*, 1 March 1907.
105 *Londonderry Sentinel*, 28 February 1907.
106 *Ibid.* 2 March 1907.
107 *Times*, 9 March 1907.
108 *Derry Journal*, 4 March 1907.
109 *Londonderry Sentinel*, 3 March 1907.
110 *Irish News*, 4 March 1907.
111 *Londonderry Sentinel*, 5 March 1907.
112 *Ibid.* 5 March 1907.
113 *Irish News*, 5 March 1907.
114 *Londonderry Sentinel*, 7 March 1907.
115 *Ibid.* 7 March 1907.
116 *Ibid.* 28 February 1907.
117 *Ibid.* 9 March 1907.
118 *Ibid.* 5 March 1907.
119 *Ibid.* 5 March 1907.
120 *Irish News*, 7 March 1907.
121 *Ibid.* 5 March 1907.
122 *Derry Journal*, 11 March 1907.
123 *Londonderry Sentinel*, 9 March 1907.
124 *Irish News*, 9 March 1907.
125 *Londonderry Sentinel*, 5 March 1907.
126 *Ibid.* 9 March 1907.
127 *Ibid.* 9 March 1907.
128 *Ibid.* 9 March 1907.
129 *Ibid.* 12 March 1907.
130 *Ibid.* 12 March 1907.
131 *Londonderry Sentinel*, 12 March 1907.
132 *Irish Weekly*, 16 March 1907.
133 *Ibid.* 16 March 1907.
134 *Londonderry Sentinel*, 14 March 1907.
135 *Derry Journal*, 11 March 1907.
136 *Ibid.* 11 March 1907.
137 *Londonderry Sentinel*, 14 March 1907.
138 *Irish News*, 14 March 1907.
139 *Irish Weekly*, 23 March 1907.
140 *Irish News*, 14 March 1907.
141 *Ibid.* 14 March 1907.

Footnotes for Chapter 2:
Parliament and Promotion, 1907-1919.

1   Interview with Sir James Henry on 29 July 1979, in London.
2   *Ibid.*
3   *Ibid.*
4   *Irish News,* 14 November 1913.
5   LR1641 *op. cit.*
6   J. Biggs-Davison and G. Chowdharey-Best *op. cit.* p292.
7   *Northern Whig,* 20 December 1909.
8   *Ibid.* 5 January 1910.
9   Unpublished Memoirs of W. E. Wylie, c. 1939-51.
10 T. J. Campbell *Fifty Years of Ulster, 1890-1940* (Belfast, 1941), p 136.
11 *Ibid.* p142.
12 *Ibid.* p143.
13 Wylie Memoirs, *op. cit.*
14 A. M. Sullivan 'Old Ireland' (London, 1927), p283.
15 *Who Was Who,* 1916-28, p928; *Who Was Who,* 1929-40, p1468; *Thom's Official Directory,* 1920, p371; *Thom's Official Directory,* 1925, p378.
16 *Irish News,* 5 January 1914.
17 *Ibid.* 1 September 1913.
18 *Irish Law Times and Solicitors' Journal,* 13 December 1913, p338.
19 *Irish News,* 8 January 1914.
20 *Ibid.* 16 February 1914; *Irish Law Times and Solicitors' Journal,* 21 February 1914, p55.
21 *Londonderry Sentinel,* 25 April 1916.
22 *Ibid.* 25 April 1916.
23 *Tyrone Constitution,* 28 April 1916.
24 *Londonderry Sentinel,* 16 May 1916.
25 *Irish News,* 20 May 1916.
26 *Ibid.* 25 May 1916.
27 B. M. Walker, *op. cit.* p363.
28 *Irish News,* 19 May 1916.
29 *Ibid.* 18 May 1916.
30 *Ibid.* 18 May 1916.
31 *Northern Whig,* 19 May 1916.
32 *Ibid.* 20 May 1916.
33 *Londonderry Sentinel,* 25 May 1916.
34 *Northern Whig,* 20 May 1916.
35 *Ibid.* 20 May 1916.
36 *Ibid.* 22 May 1916.
37 *Irish News,* 23 May 1916.
38 *Ibid.* 23 May 1916.
39 *Ibid.* 23 May 1916.
40 *Londonderry Sentinel,* 25 May 1916.
41 *Ibid.* 25 May 1916.
42 *Irish News,* 24 May 1916.
43 Henry Family papers.
44 *Londonderry Sentinel,* 25 May 1916.
45 *Northern Whig,* 30 May 1916.
46 D. Kiberd '*1916 Rebellion Handbook*' (Mourne River Press, 1998), p213.
47 *Ibid.* p214.
48 *Ibid.* p213.
49 *Ibid.* p214.
50 *Ibid.* p215.
51 *Ibid.* p216.
52 *Ibid.* p217.
53 *Ibid.* p218.
54 *Ibid.* p219.
55 J. McColgan '*British Policy and the Irish Administration, 1920-22.*' (London, 1983) p6
56 *Ibid.* p7
57 L. McBride '*The Greening of Dublin Castle*' (1991) p224.
58 *Ibid.* p229.
59 *Ibid.* p229.
60 *Who Was Who,* 1916-1928, p928.
61 L. McBride *op. cit.* pp242-243.
62 J. R. B. McMinn *Against The Tide: Papers of Rev. J. B. Armour Presbyterian Minister and Protestant Home Ruler* (PRONI, 1985), 176.
63 L. McBride *op. cit.* p251.
64 *Irish Law Times and Solicitors' Journal,* 30 November 1918, p291.
65 *Northern Whig,* 20 May 1919.
66 *Ibid.* 18 June 1919.
67 *Irish Weekly,* 9 November 1918.
68 *Ulster Guardian,* 2 November 1918.
69 *Irish Weekly,* 23 November 1918.
70 *Ibid.* 23 November 1918.
71 *Northern Whig,* 19 November 1918.
72 *Ulster Guardian,* 30 November 1918.

73 *Northern Constitution,* 7 December 1918.

74 *Ibid.* 23 November 1918.

75 *Northern Whig,* 6 November 1918.

76 *Londonderry Sentinel,* 12 November 1918.

77 Quoted in *Londonderry Sentinel,* 30 November 1918.

78 *Ibid.* 23 November 1918.

79 *Northern Constitution,* 7 December 1918.

80 *Ibid.* 7 December 1918 and 14 December 1918.

81 *Irish Weekly,* 7 December 1918.

82 *Northern Constitution,* 14 December 1918.

83 *Ibid.* 7 December 1918.

84 *Northern Whig,* 6 December 1918.

85 *Northern Constitution,* 7 December 1918.

86 *Ibid.* 14 December 1918.

87 *Coleraine Chronicle,* 28 September 1918.

88 *Ibid.* 28 September 1918.

89 *Northern Whig,* 6 December 1918.

90 *Ibid.* 6 December 1918.

91 *Ibid.* 10 December 1918.

92 *Coleraine Chronicle,* 7 December 1918.

93 *Northern Constitution,* 14 December 1918.

94 *Irish News,* 13 July 1984.

95 *Coleraine Chronicle,* 14 December 1918.

96 *Northern Whig,* 10 December 1918.

97 *Northern Constitution,* 14 December 1918.

98 *Coleraine Chronicle,* 14 December 1918.

99 *Northern Constitution,* 7 December 1918.

100 *Coleraine Chronicle,* 14 December 1918.

101 *Northern Constitution,* 21 December 1918.

102 *Strabane Chronicle,* 21 December 1918.

103 *Derry Journal,* 16 December 1918.

104 *Coleraine Chronicle,* 21 December 1918.

105 *Northern Constitution,* 21 December 1918.

106 *Ibid.* 4 January 1919.

Footnotes for Chapter 3:
Parliamentary career of Denis Henry, 1916-1921 (I)

1   J. Casey *The Irish Law Officers* (Round Hall Sweet and Maxwell, 1996), p28.
2   *Ibid.* pp 36-37.
3   *Banbridge Chronicle,* 7 December 1918.
4   *County Down Spectator,* 16 November 1918.
5   J. Casey *op. cit.* p42.
6   *Ibid.* p48
7   *Ibid.* p37.
8   L. O'Broin *W. E. Wylie and the Irish Revolution* (Dublin, 1989) pp54-55.
9   G. A. Hayes-McCoy 'The Conduct of the Anglo-Irish War, January 1919- July 1921', p58 in *'The Irish Struggle, 1916-1926'* , D. Williams (London, 1968)
10 G. A. Hayes-McCoy *op. cit.* p58
11 W. A. Philips *'The Revolution in Ireland, 1906-1923'* (London, 1923) p174
12 E. Holt 'Protest in Arms: the Irish Troubles 1916-1923' (London, 1960) p 191.
13 W. A. Philips *op. cit.* p174.
14 C. Townshend *'The British Campaign in Ireland, 1919-1921'* (Oxford, 1975) pp65-69.
15 E. Holt *op. cit.* p218.
16 D. Macardle *'The Irish Republic'* (Dublin, 1951) p348.
17 *Ibid.* p344.
18 *Irish News,* 13 April 1920.
19 5 HC DEB 127 (12 April 1920) 1487
20 *Ibid.* 1489-1490.
21 *Irish News,* 13 April 1920
22 5 HC DEB 127 (13 April 1920) 1532-1543.
23 *Ibid.* 1564
24 *Ibid.* 1561-1565.
25 *Irish News,* 14 April 1920.
26 *Belfast Newsletter,* 14 April 1920.
27 5 HC DEB 127 (13 April 1920) 1644.
28 *Ibid.* 1646.
29 *Irish News,* 14 April 1920.
30 *Belfast Newsletter,* 15 April 1920.
31 *Ibid.* 15 April 1920.

32 C. J. C. Street *The Administration in Ireland, 1920* (London, 1921) p83.
33 *Times,* 14 April 1920.
34 T. Jones *Whitehall Diary – Vol 3 Ireland 1918-1925,* ed. by K. Middlemas (London, 1971) p15.
35 5 HC DEB 127 (13 April 1920) 1546.
36 *Ibid.* 1646.
37 J. C. Beckett *The Making of Modern Ireland 1603-1923* (London, 1971) p448.
38 HC DEB 125 (16 February 1920) 602.
39 5 HC DEB 129 (20 May 1920) 1731.
40 D. Macardle *op. cit.* p348.
41 5 HC DEB (19 February 1920) 1171.
42 5 HC DEB (16 February 1920) 601-602.
43 5 HC DEB (19 February 1920) 1147.
44 *Ibid.* 1169-1170.
45 5 HC DEB (16 February 1920) 601.
46 *Ibid.* 580.
47 5 HC DEB (19 February 1920) 1175.
48 *Ibid.* 1149.
49 *Irish News,* 17 February 1920.
50 *Ibid.* 17 February 1920.
51 *Ibid.* 20 February 1920.
52 C. J. C. Street *op. cit.* p97.
53 D. Macardle *op. cit.* p362.
54 T. Jones *op. cit.* p17.
55 *Ibid.* p19.
56 *Ibid.* p19.
57 *Ibid.* p20.
58 *Ibid.* p62.
59 *Ibid.* p33.
60 C. J. C. Street *op. cit.* p411.
61 C. Younger *'Ireland's Civil War'* (London, 1968) p104.
62 5 HC DEB 132 (6 August 1920) 2883.
63 *Ibid.* 2930.
64 *Irish News,* 7 August 1920.
65 5 HC DEB 132 (6 August 1920) 2909-2914.
66 C. Townshend *op. cit.* pp97-98.
67 *Ibid.* p101.
68 L. O'Broin *op. cit.* p81.
69 *Ibid.* p118

70   *Ibid.* p105.

71   *Ibid.* p96.

72   T. Jones op. cit p59.

73   *Ibid.* p63.

74   C. Campbell *Emergency Law in Ireland, 1918-1923* (Oxford, 1994) pp97-98.

75   *Ibid.* p99.

76   *Irish News,* 6 May 1921.

77   5 HC DEB 141 (5 May 1921) 1204.

78   5 HC DEB 141 (13 May 1921) 2392-2407.

79   *Irish News,* 6 May 1921.

80   5 HC DEB 141 (5 May 1921) 1204-1206.

81   5 HC DEB 141 (13 May 1921) 2392-2407.

82   J. Biggs-Davison and G. Chowdharry-Best *op. cit* p325.

83   5 HC DEB 128 (19 April 1920) 189-190.

84   5 HC DEB 135 (2 December 1920) 1415-1416.

85   *Ibid.* 2389-2390.

86   *Ibid.* 2390.

87   5 HC DEB 132 (22 July 1920) 792.

88   5 HC DEB 138 (24 March 1921) 2748 .

89   *Belfast Newsletter,* 23 June 1920.

90   5 HC DEB 130 (22 June 1920) 2013.

91   *Ibid.* 2126.

92   *Ibid.* 2127.

93   *Irish News,* 23 June 1920.

94   Quoted in *Belfast Newsletter,* 24 June 1920.

95   *Ibid.* 23 June 1920.

96   *Irish News,* 1 December 1920.

97   5 HC DEB 129 (20 May 1920) 1739-1740.

98   *Ibid.* 1740.

99   5 HC DEB 132 (22 July 1920) 789-790.

100 *Ibid.* 777.

101 *Ibid.* 790.

102 *Ibid.* 790.

103 5 HC DEB 134 (5 November 1920) 738-739.

104 *Ibid.* 739.

105 *Ibid.* 742.

106 *Ibid.* 744.

107 Henry Family Papers.

108 *Ibid.*

109 *Ibid.*

110 5 HC DEB 134 (10 November 1920) 1237-1239.

111 5 HC DEB 130 (23 June 1920) 2557-2558.

112 *Ibid.* 2557.

113 *Ibid.* 2577.

114 *Ibid.* 2580.

Footnotes for Chapter 4:
Parliamentary Career of Denis Henry, 1916-1921 (II)

1 5 HC DEB 120 (27 October 1919) 408.
2 *Ibid.* 408.
3 5 HC DEB 1210 (31 October 1919) 1075-1076.
4 5 HC DEB 122 (9 December 1919) 1235-1238.
5 *Ibid.* 1252.
6 5 HC DEB 120 (31 October 1919) 1079.
7 5 HC DEB 118 (18 July 1919) 844-845 .
8 5 HC DEB 118 (1 August 1919) 2479-2489.
9 5 HC DEB 128 (29 April 1920) 1387-1388.
10 5 HC DEB 131 (28 June 1920) 59.
11 5 HC DEB 130 (11 June 1920) 2189-2190.
12 5 HC DEB 129 (3 June 1920) 2189-2190.
13 5 HC DEB 130 (24 June 1920) 2391 and (24 June 1920) 2350.
14 5 HC DEB (10 June 1920) 575.
15 Interview with Sir James Henry, on 20 July 1979, in London.
16 Henry Family Papers.

Footnotes for Chapter 5:
Lord Chief Justice of Northern Ireland, 1921-1925.

1 F. Newark *The Law and the Constitution in Ulster under Home Rule*, ed. T. Wilson (London, 1955) p44.

2 N. Mansergh *The Government of Northern Ireland* (London, 1936) p264.

3 F. Newark *op. cit.* p44.

4 *Ibid.* p44.

5 *Londonderry Sentinel*, 18 June 1921.

6 *Irish News*, 14 May 1921.

7 *Ibid.* 14 May 1921.

8 *Londonderry Sentinel*, 31 May 1921.

9 *Ibid.* 7 June 1921.

10 *Ibid.* 2 June 1921.

11 *Belfast Newsletter*, 6 August 1921.

12 *Londonderry Sentinel*, 6 August 1921.

13 Henry Family Papers.

14 *Londonderry Sentinel*, 9 June 1921.

15 J. Biggs-Davison and G. Chowdharay-best *op. cit.* p355.

16 *Northern Whig*, 6 August 1921.

17 Henry Family Papers.

18 *Ibid.*

19 *Ibid.*

20 Quoted in *Irish News*, 6 August 1921.

21 *Belfast Newsletter*, 6 August 1921.

22 *Irish News*, 6 August 1921.

23 Henry Family Papers.

24 *Belfast Newsletter*, 6 August 1921.

25 *Belfast Telegraph*, 1 October 1921.

26 *Londonderry Sentinel* 11 August 1921 and *Belfast Newsletter*, 9 August 1921.

27 *Irish News*, 10 August 1921.

28 *Belfast Telegraph*, 15 august 1921.

29 *Northern Whig*, 12 August 1921.

30 *Ibid.* 30 August 1921.

31 *Ibid.* 26 august 1921.

32 *Belfast Telegraph*, 1 October 1921.

33 *Ibid.* 1 October 1921.

34 *Ibid.* 1 October 1921.

35 *Ibid.* 1 October 1921.

36 L. J. Jones *His Life and Times: the Autobiography of the Rt. Honourable Sir Edward Jones* (Enniskillen, 1987) p43 and p91.

37 *Belfast Telegraph*, 1 October 1921.

38 *Belfast and Ulster Directory, 1925.*

39 *The Incorporated Law Society's Calendar and Law Directory, 1920* (Dublin, 1920) p207.

40 *Belfast Telegraph*, 1 October 1921.

41 T. J. Campbell *Between the Wars* quoted in *Belfast: Origin and Growth of an Industrial City*, ed. J. C. Beckett and R. Glasscock (London, 1971) p146.

42 H. Shearman *Northern Ireland 1921-1971* (HMSO, 1971) p24.

43 P. Buckland *Irish Unionism 2: Ulster Unionism and the origins of Northern Ireland 1886-1922* (Dublin, 1973) p170.

44 P. Buckland *Irish Unionism 2 op. cit.* p176

45 H. Shearman *op. cit.* p24.

46 T. J. Campbell *Belfast between the Wars op. cit.* p147

47 H. Shearman *op. cit.* p23.

48 P. Buckland *Irish Unionism 2 op. cit.* p159.

49 L. de Paor *Divided Ulster* 9 London, 1977) p100.

50 P. Buckland *Irish Unionism 2 op. cit.* p165.

51 *Ibid.* p158.

52 H. Shearman *op. cit.* p25.

53 P. Buckland *Irish Unionism 2 op. cit* p172.

54 L. de Paor *op. cit.* p102.

55 P. Buckland *Irish Unionism 2 op. cit.* p155.

56 *Ibid.* p150.

57 T. J. Campbell *Fifty years of Ulster op. cit.* p105.

58 P. Buckland *Irish Unionism 2 op. cit.* p153.

59 PRONI CAB6/57: Publication of Memorandum on Supreme Court of Judicature, by Lord Justice Moore 1 October 1921-31 July 1922. *

Hereafter footnoted as PRONI CAB6/57:

60 PRONI CAB6/57: *Ibid.*
61 PRONI CAB6/57: *Ibid.* p30.
62 PRONI CAB6/57: p1.
63 PRONI CAB6/57: *Ibid.* p1.
64 PRONI CAB6/57: *Ibid.* p1.
65 *Belfast Telegraph,* 1 October 1921.
66 PRONI CAB6/57: *Ibid.* p1.
67 PRONI CAB6/57: *Ibid.* p1.
68 PRONI CAB9B/17/2:Report of Departmental Committee on the Jury System of Northern Ireland pp78-79.
69 PRONI CAB6/57: *Ibid.* p2.
70 PRONI CAB6/57: *Ibid.* p2.
71 PRONI CAB6/57: *Ibid.* p2.
72 PRONI CAB6/57: *Ibid.* p3.
73 PRONI CAB6/57: *Ibid.* p3.
74 PRONI CAB6/57: *Ibid.* p3.
75 PRONI CAB6/57: *Ibid.* p3.
76 PRONI CAB6/57: *Ibid.* p3.
77 PRONI CAB6/57: *Ibid.* p4.
78 *Belfast Telegraph,* 25 October 1921.
79 PRONI CAB6/57: *Ibid.* p4.
80 PRONI CAB9B/17/2: Report of Departmental committee on the Jury System of Northern Ireland
81 T. J. Campbell *Fifty Years of Ulster op. cit.* p109.
82 PRONI CAB4/1407: 23 April 1925.
83 PRONI CAB6/57: *Ibid.* pp4-5.
84 PRONI CAB6/57: *Ibid.* p5.
85 PRONI CAB6/57: *Ibid.* p5.
86 H. Shearman *op. cit.* p20.
87 PRONI CAB6/57: *Ibid.* p6.
88 PRONI CAB6/57: *Ibid.* p7.
89 PRONI CAB6/57: *Ibid.* p7.
90 PRONI CAB6/57: *Ibid.* p7.
91 *Belfast Telegraph,* 21 October 1921.
92 PRONI CAB6/57: *Ibid.* p6
93 PRONI CAB6/57: *Ibid.* p6.
94 PRONI CAB6/57: *Ibid.* p9.
95 PRONI CAB6/57: *Ibid.* pp7-8.
96 PRONI CAB6/57: *Ibid.* p8.
97 PRONI CAB6/57: *Ibid.* p9.
98 PRONI CAB6/57: *Ibid.* pp23-24.
99 PRONI CAB6/57: *Ibid.* p17.
100 PRONI CAB6/57: *Ibid.* pp17-18.
101 PRONI CAB6/57: *Ibid.* p9.
102 PRONI CAB6/57: *Ibid.* p18.

103 PRONI CAB6/57: *Ibid.* p11.
104 PRONI CAB6/57: *Ibid.* p11.
105 PRONI CAB6/57: *Ibid.* p12.
106 PRONI CAB6/57: *Ibid.* p23.
107 PRONI CAB6/57: *Ibid.* p25.
108 PRONI CAB6/57: *Ibid.* pp12-13.
109 PRONI CAB6/57: Report of Departmental Committee on the Jury System of Northern Ireland p29.
110 PRONI CAB6/57: *Ibid.* p13.
111 PRONI CAB6/57: *Ibid.* p19.
112 PRONI CAB6/57: *Ibid.* p20
113 PRONI CAB6/57: *Ibid.* p28.
114 PRONI CAB6/57: *Ibid.* p27.
115 PRONI CAB6/57: *Ibid.* p27.
116 C. Campbell op.cit. p334.
117 *Irish Law Times Report, 56, 170, 1922.*
118 *Irish News,* 18 July 1922.
119 C. Campbell *op. cit.* p335 and *Irish Law Times Report, 56. 170, 1922.*
120 *Irish News,* 18 July 1922.
121 PRONI CAB8B/11: File on Cushendall Ambush (PRONI).
122 *Ibid.* 18 July 1922.
123 *Ibid.* 20 July 1922.
124 *Ibid.* 3 August 1922.
125 P. Bew, P. Gibbon and H. Patterson *The State of Northern Ireland, 1921-1972* (Manchester, 1989) p72.
126 B. Farrell *Arming the Protestants* (Brandon, 1983) pp164-165.
127 PRONI CAB8B / 11: 22 November 1922.
128 *Ibid:* 24 January 1923.
129 B. Farrell *op. cit.* p165.
130 *Irish News,* 1 November 1923.
131 L. J. Jones *op. cit.* p96.
132 *Irish News,* 1 November 1923.
133 PRONI CAB8B / 11: Henry's ruling on Cushendall Ambush.
134 D 1507 / F / 11 / 1-16: Carson's visit to Belfast in October 1923.
135 PRONI CAB9D / 9 / 1: Correspondence relating to Henry's nomination as a Senator for Queen's University Belfast, 23 October 1924.
136 *Ibid.:* 8 November 1924.
137 *Ibid.:* 11 November 1924.

138 Interview with Sir James Henry, on 29 July 1979, in London.

139 PRONI CAB4/48/11: The subject was discussed at a PRONI Cabinet meeting, 19-20 June 1922.

140 PRONI CAB9B/17/2: Report of Departmental Committee on the Jury System of Northern Ireland p61.

141 PRONI CAB4/79/6: PRONI Cabinet discussion on 27 April 1925.

142 PRONI CAB6/57: *Ibid.* p27.

143 PRONI CAB6/57: *Ibid.* p28.

144 PRONI CAB6/57: p29

145 PRONI CAB6/57: Letter from Moore to Craig, 9 October 1922.

146 PRONI CAB6/57: Letter from Magill to Spender, 4 November 1922.

147 PRONI CAB6/57: Spender to Magill, 14 November 1922.

148 PRONI CAB6/57: Spender to Denis Henry, 28 November 1922.

Footnotes for Chapter 6:
Conclusions on the life of Denis Henry

1   *Strabane Chronicle*, 3 October 1925.
2   *Irish News*, 2 October 1925.
3   *Londonderry Sentinel*, 3 October 1925.
4   *Irish News*, 5 October 1925.
5   M. Stenton and S. Lees *Who's Who of British members of Parliament*, Vol. IV, 1945-1979 (Sussex, 1981) p127.
6   *Irish News*, 2 October 1925.
7   *Times*, 2 October 1925.
8   *Londonderry Sentinel*, 3 October 1925.
9   *Irish Law Times and Solicitors' Journal*, 3 October 1925, p239.
10   Henry Family Papers.
11   *Ibid.*
12   St. John Ervine quoted in J. Biggs-Davison and G. Chowdharay-Best *op. cit.* p355.
13   J. Ross *Pilgrim Script: More Reminiscences* (London 1927), p127
14   G. Hill Smith *The Supreme Court of Judicature of Northern Ireland* (Belfast 1926), p34
15   *Ibid.* pp35-36.
16   *Ibid.* pp38-39.
17   *Times*, 2 October 1925.
18   R. McNeill *Ulster's Stand for Union* (London, 1922) p35.
19   J. R. B. McMinn *op. cit.* p183.
20   *Londonderry Sentinel*, 3 October 1925.
21   D. Curran *The Story of St. Paul's Belfast outline* (Belfast, 1987) p68.
22   Henry Family Papers.
23   *Incorporated Law Society's Calendar and Law Directory 1920* (Dublin, 1920) p245.
24   *Ibid.* p243.
25   J. Biggs-Davison and G. Chowdharay-Best *op. cit.* p291.
26   J. Ross *op. cit.* p128.
27   *Londonderry Sentinel*, 3 October 1925.
28   *Irish Times*, 3 October 1925.
29   F. Callanan *Tim Healy* (Cork, 1996) p627

30   T. M. Healy *Letters and Leaders of My Day* (Thornton-Butterworth, 1928) p 587.
31   *Ibid.* p571.
32   *Ibid.* p643.
33   *Ibid.* p571.
34   *Ibid.* p575.
35   *Belfast Telegraph*, 2 October 1925.
36   M. Healy *The Old Munster Circuit* (1935) p35.
37   *Belfast Telegraph*, 2 October 1925.
38   L. J. Jones *op. cit.* p91.
39   *Northern Whig*, 2 October 1925.
40   M. Healy *op. cit.* p93.
41   R. B. McDowell *The Fate of the Southern Unionists: Crisis and Decline* (Lilliput, 1997) p2.
42   *Ibid.* p3.
43   J. Biggs-Davison and G/ Chowdharay-Best *op. cit.* p248.
44   R. B. McDowell *op. cit.* p2.
45   *Ibid.* pp3-4.
46   J. Biggs-Davison and G. Chowdharay-Best *op. cit.* pp246-248.
47   *Belfast Telegraph*, 2 October 1925.
48   M. Sturgis *The Last Days of Dublin Castle: The Mark Sturgis Diaries* ed. by M. Hopkinson (Dublin, 1999) p110.
49   *Ibid.* p110.
50   *Ibid.* p111.
51   *Ibid.* pp115-116.
52   *Northern Constitution*, 5 November 1921.
53   J. Biggs-Davison and G. Chowdharay-Best *op. cit.* p374.
54   *Ibid.* p377.
55   *Ibid.* p379.
56   *Ibid.* p390.
57   Henry Family Papers.

BIBLIOGRAPHY

1 SECONDARY SOURCES:

BECKETT, J. C. 'The Making of Modern Ireland, 1603-1923'. (London, 1971.

BEW, P; GIBBON P AND PATTERSON H. 'The State of Northern Ireland, 1921-72'. (Manchester, 1989).

BIGGS-DAVISON J. AND CHOWDHARRY-BEST, G 'The Cross of St. Patrick: The Catholic Unionist Tradition in Ireland' (Kensal, 1984).

BUCKLAND, P. 'Irish Unionism, 1885-1923' (Belfast, 1973)

BUCKLAND, P. 'Irish Unionism 2: Ulster Unionism and the Origins of Northern Ireland, 1886-1922'. (Dublin, 1973)

CALLANAN, F. 'Tim Healy' (Cork, 1996)

CAMPBELL, C. 'Emergency Law in Ireland, 1918-25' (Oxford, 1994).

CAMPBELL, T. J. 'Fifty Years of Ulster, 1890-1940' (Belfast, 1941).

CAMPBELL, T. J. 'Between the Wars', in 'Belfast: Origin and Growth of an Industrial city', ed. By Beckett, J. C. and Glasscock, R.

CASEY, J. 'The Irish Law Officers' (Round Hall Sweet and Maxwell, 1996).

Curran, D. 'The Story of St. Paul's Belfast' (Belfast, 1987).

DE PAOR, L. 'Divided Ulster' (London, 1977).

FARRELL, B. 'Arming the Protestants(Brandon, 1983).

HAYES-McCOY, G. A. 'The Conduct of the Anglo-Irish War, January 1919-July 1921', in Williams, T. D. 'The Irish Struggle, 1916-1926' (London, 1968)

HEALY, M. 'The Old Munster Circuit' (1935)

HEALY, T. 'Letters and Leaders of My Day' (Thornton and Butterworth, 1928)

HILL SMITH, G. 'The Supreme Court of Judiciature of Northern Ireland' (Belfast, 1926).

HOLT, E. 'Protest in Arms: The Irish Troubles, 1916 0 1923' (London, 1960).

JONES, L. J. 'His Life and Times: The Autobiography of the Rt. Hon. Sir Edward Jones'. (Enniskillen, 1987)

JONES, T. 'Whitehall Diary – Vol. 3, Ireland 1918-1923', ed by Middlemas, K (London, 1971).

KIBERD, D. '1916 Rebellion Handbook' (Mourne River Press, 1998).

MacARDLE, D. 'The Irish Republic' (Dublin, 1951).

McBRIDE, L. 'The Greening of Dublin Castle' (1991)

McCOLGAN, J. 'British Policy and the Irish Administration, 1920-1922' (London, 1983).

McDOWELL, R. B. 'The Fate of the Southern Unionists: Crisis and Decline' (Lilliput, 1997).

McMINN, J. R. B. 'Against the Tide: Papers of Rev. J. B. Armour' (PRONI, 1985)

McNEILL, R. 'Ulster's Stand for Union' (London, 1922).

MANSERGH, N. 'The Government of Northern Ireland' (London, 1936).

NEWARK, F. 'The Law and the Constitution in Ulster under Home Rule', ed. Wilson, T (London, 1955).

O'BROIN, L. 'W. E. Wylie and the Irish Revolution, 1916-1921' (Dublin, 1989).

PHILIPS, W. A. 'The Revolution in Ireland, 1906-1923' (London, 1923).

ROSS, J. 'Pilgrim Script: More Reminiscences' (London 1927).

SHEARMAN, H. 'Northern Ireland, 1921-1971' (HMSO, 1971).

STENTON, M. AND LEES, S. (Eds) 'Who's Who of British Members of Parliament, Vol. IV, 1945-1979' (Sussex, 1981).

STREET, C. J. C. 'The Administration in Ireland, 1920' (London, 1921).

STURGIS, M. 'The Last Days of Dublin Castle: the Mark Sturgis Diaries' ed by M. Hopkinson (Dublin, 1999).

TOWNSHEND, C. 'The British Campaign in Ireland, 1919-1921' (Oxford, 1975).

2 NEWSPAPERS:

> *Banbridge Chronicle*
> *Belfast Newsletter*
> *Belfast Telegraph*
> *County Down Spectator*
> *Coleraine Chronicle*
> *Derry Journal*
> *Impartial Reporter*
> *Irish News*
> *Irish Times*
> *Irish Weekly*
> *Londonderry Sentinel*
> *Northern Constitution*
> *Northern Whig*
> *Strabane Chronicle*
> *Times*
> *Tyrone Constitution*
> *Ulster Guardian*

3 DOCUMENTS IN THE PUBLIC RECORDS OFFICE OF NORTHERN IRELAND

CAB/4 /48 /11:

Cabinet discussion mentions Denis Henry as a possible temporary replacement for the Lord Lieutenant, Fitz Alan (19-20 June 1922)

CAB/4/79 /6:

Denis Henry consulted over nominations for the Pensions Appeal Tribunal (April, 1925)

CAB/4/140 /7:

Minister of Labour expresses concern with the progress of the new Law Courts' Building (April 1925)

CAB/6/57:

Publication of Memorandum on Supreme Court of Judicature, by Lord Justice Moore, 1 October 1921-31 July 1922.

CAB/8/B/11:

File on Cushendall Ambush

CAB/9D/9/11:

Correspondence relating to Denis Henry's nomination as a Senator for Queen's University, Belfast, 1924.

D/1507/F/11/1-16:

Carson Papers: Visit to Belfast, October 1923.

D/1507/F/11/11:

Photograph of Denis Henry with Carson and others, October 1923.

D/2298/16/1:

Letters held by Wilson and Simms, solicitors, Strabane.

LR/141:

Will of James Henry and family members.

SCH/665/1/1:

Records of Draperstown National School for Boys, 1870-1903.

4 OTHER SOURCES;

Hansard

Henry Family Papers

Interview with Sir James Henry, on 29 July 1979, in London

The Incorporated Law Society's Calendar and Law Directory for 1920

Irish Law Times and Solicitors' Journal

Irish Law Times Reports

Mount St. Mary's College archives

Thom's Official Directory

Unpublished Memoirs of W.E. Wylie

Who Was Who

INDEX

155